HOW THE BIBLE CAN HELP US UNDERSTAND

ILLNESS, DISABILITY AND CARING

T0155394

HOW THE BIBLE CAN HELP US UNDERSTAND

ILLNESS, DISABILITY AND CARING

A Bible study for individuals or groups

BERNADETTE MEADEN

DARTON · LONGMAN + TODD

First published in 2020 by
Darton, Longman and Todd
1 Spencer Court
140 – 142 Wandsworth High Street
London SW18 4JJ

Print book ISBN: 978-0-232-53456-6
Ebook ISBN:978-0-232-53457-3

A catalogue record for this book is available
from the British Library

Designed and produced by Judy Linard

CONTENTS

SERIES
INTRODUCTION

The Bible is the collection of writings and prayers pulled together by people and prophets over a period spanning approximately fifteen centuries[1] to describe humanity's relationship with God. It has great value for the three monotheistic religions, Judaism, Christianity and Islam, but as the key text of Christianity it plays a particularly vital role in the lives of Christians. Originally communicated orally, the written words of the Bible reflect the history, culture and theological understanding of the times in which they were written. In some instances, this can lead to contradictions, confusion and disagreements about its meaning. Nonetheless, the search for answers and collective wisdom found in the Bible's pages continue to make it highly relevant for the world we live in today.

The Jerusalem Bible was first published in 1956 by French scholars at the École Biblique in Jerusalem, in response to Pope Pius XII's encyclical suggesting a translation from Greek and Hebrew texts. In 1966, Darton, Longman and Todd published an English version of the Jerusalem Bible, using the French text as the basis. This version was edited by Alexander Jones and included contributions from well-known Catholics such as J. R. R. Tolkien, and has always been praised for its literary qualities. Nineteen years later the New Jerusalem Bible edited by Dom Henry Wansbrough was published. Translated directly from the Greek and Hebrew, it incorporated new scholarship, fresh study material and the experience of two decades of use in churches. In 2019, Darton, Longman and Todd published the Revised New Jerusalem Bible, also translated by Dom Henry. This significantly changed version comes complete with updated study notes and inclusive language. It is one of the first new translations of the Bible in the twenty-first century and has been widely praised.

To celebrate the launch of the Revised New Jerusalem Bible, Darton, Longman Todd have commissioned this series of study guides to the Bible. Recognising how much the Bible can teach us today and using the RNJB as the translation for the text, each book will take an aspect of life and ask how the Bible can help us understand it better. Each book will be written by a Catholic who will bring their own perspective to the subject matter. The authors are drawn from lay and religious, people with theological training and those without. Where many Bible Study Guides are written by Bible experts, this series is taking a different approach. Each author has been commissioned to write from their unique lived experience, using their personal response to key Bible passages to throw a light on the topic under discussion, reinforcing the intent of the

Revised New Jerusalem Bible to be a Bible for 'study and proclamation'.

HOW TO USE THESE STUDY GUIDES

The format of these study guides is very simple. There will be a brief introduction to the topic, followed by 5 or 6 chapters picking up a key theme, leading to a concluding chapter. Each book is short enough to read in one sitting so you may find benefit from reading it through once before you start using it for study, and then focussing on one chapter at a time. You may wish to take notes as you go, to help with your reflections. Each book is designed to be read either privately or as part of a small study group.

1. Read the chapter through to gain an understanding of the author's arguments. Have a think about what they are saying, do you agree, do you disagree? Have you seen something in a different light?
2. Re-read again, focussing on the Bible passages referred to. Are the texts familiar to you? What do you think of the author's interpretation? Do you have an alternative one? Is this helpful to your life?
3. Each chapter is broken into sections with questions for you to reflect on. Use them as a springboard for further thought and your own independent study of the Bible.
4. The author's ideas and interpretations on the biblical texts cited are their own. Readers may not agree with every position

taken, but it is hoped that these guides will help provoke thought and deepen your own understanding of the issues.

5. Follow the recommended actions and review afterwards whether it has helped or hindered your understanding.

6. Use the final prayer and the Bible texts referred to in the chapter to pray about the issues highlighted.

7. If undertaking this guide as a group, please do consider how you might ensure you are accessible to everyone. This could include welcoming housebound people to participate via Zoom, inviting people from every community in the parish, and ensuring it is at a time to suit parents and carers.

Virginia Moffatt
Series Editor

NOTES

1. *When was the Bible Written?*, International Bible Society Website: https://www.biblica.com/resources/bible-faqs/when-was-the-bible-written/

2. Denise Cottrell-Boyce, *How the Bible Can Help Us Understand Welcoming the Stranger* (Darton, Longman and Todd, 2020).

INTRODUCTION

Illness, disability, and caring are aspects of life which will affect all of us in some way at some time. Whether we are born with a disability or chronic health condition, or acquire one later, very few of us will reach the end of our lives without experiencing any illness or disability. As far as caring is concerned, most of us will have a parent, partner or family member who at some point needs care – so this is a topic which to a greater or lesser extent affects all of us.

I was born with a rare form of complex congenital heart disease, so have experienced some limitations and challenges in my life which I hope helps me to understand some of the issues explored in this book – but of course, every person is unique and every illness and disability affects people differently. Most areas of disability or illness are as unfamiliar to me as they are to anyone else who hasn't experienced them. So, I make no claim to expertise on the issues explored in this book, or, indeed, on theology. What follows is very much a personal view, and simply offered as a starting point for thinking and discussion. The hope is that through such discussion, the knowledge and experiences available will be multiplied. Everyone will have something unique to contribute, and thus the discussions will certainly contain far more insight than the book.

People who experience illness and disability, or who are caring for people, can find life a constant struggle, not just because of the difficulties caused by their own particular challenges but also because of a society, an economy, and a built environment which often shows little consideration for their needs and requirements.

With this in mind, the aim of the book is twofold. First, to explore how we can use the wisdom and inspiration we find in the Bible to help us deal with the personal challenges we may all encounter at some stage in our lives. Second, to use the message of the Bible to think about how we can make a society which is better and fairer for everybody, and which will enable more people to live a happy, fulfilling and rewarding life.

The way disability is talked about in much of the Bible is not the way we would talk about it in the twenty-first century. Using blindness or deafness as metaphors for a lack of perception, for instance, would rightly be condemned today. But to focus on this is, I believe, to miss the beautiful bigger picture. Above everything soars the radically inclusive love offered and modelled by Jesus, who seeks out those who have been pushed to the margins of society, and embraces those who have been excluded. If we follow the example of this radically inclusive love, we will automatically seek justice and respect for everybody, with nobody excluded or demeaned.

I hope this comes through as the overarching theme of this book.

We will begin by looking at the idea that illness or disability can be some kind of punishment from God, or can make people in some way less worthy. This is a view found mostly in the Old Testament, but by looking at several accounts of healing in the gospels we can see that Jesus completely rejects that view. Particularly important is the story of the man born blind who is healed by Jesus in John's gospel.

Next we will look at how society can be organised in a way that is more consistent with the idea that we are all made in God's image, and so are all equally precious and deserving of a decent life. An important parable here is the story of the labourers in the vineyard, from Matthew's gospel.

In the third chapter we will consider the concepts of weakness and strength, and how suffering can give people authority. Paul's first letter to the Corinthians explains how, for Christians, the crucifixion has redefined our understanding of strength and success.

Next we will explore suffering itself, how we understand it and how we cope with it. We will look at Jesus' solidarity with our suffering, because he too went through pain and anguish, and explore the role of prayer. We will consider Jesus in the Garden of Gethsemane, and Paul's assertion in his letter to the Romans that nothing can separate us from the love of God.

In the fifth chapter we will look at the role of carers, both paid and unpaid. An important parable here is the story of the Good Samaritan, followed by Jesus' visit to Martha and Mary. We will look at how the caring role can be a gift, but it can also be an almost overwhelming challenge, and how it is not just a personal responsibility but also a social responsibility.

In the last chapter, we will explore the tendency to regard some aspects of ill health as a form of moral failing, and look at how inequality can be an enormous influence on how healthy we are, or how long we live. Here we will look at the parable of the Pharisee and the tax collector in Luke's gospel, and the way in which early Christian communities modelled a fairer society, in Acts.

With the radical inclusiveness of Jesus in mind, I would ask anyone who is planning to organise group sessions using this book to think about making them as accessible as possible. Are there people who would like to take part, but could only do so if transport were provided? Are there people who are housebound or bedbound, but would be happy to host one or more sessions in their own home? Can you make use of Zoom?

It should also be said that some of the subject matter in the book may have a particularly personal relevance for some members of a group, who may find it upsetting to participate in some discussions. It might therefore be good to give people advance notice of what will be talked about, so they have the opportunity not to take part in certain sessions if they wish, with no questions asked.

I also need to mention terminology. While some people prefer 'people with a disability', others take the view that the term 'disabled people' better reflects the social model of disability. The Mental Health Foundation explains the social model thus:

> 'It is a civil rights approach to disability. If modern life was set up in a way that was accessible for people with disabilities then they would not be excluded or restricted. The distinction is made between 'impairments', which are the individual problems which may prevent people from doing something, and "disability", which is the additional disadvantage bestowed by a society which treats these "impairments" as abnormal, thus unnecessarily excluding these people from full participation in society. The social model of disability says that it is society which disables impaired people.'[1]

So, for simplicity and readability, I will use the term 'disabled people' to refer to people with either a static impairment, or with a physical or mental illness or condition which makes everyday life more of a challenge. I hope this is acceptable and apologise in advance for any unintentional lack of sensitivity or understanding.

Finally, this book was originally completed before the COVID-19 pandemic began to affect the UK, in what felt like a very different time. Some late changes were made to reflect the developing situation, but at the time those changes were made it was still unclear what the impact of the virus would be, or how society may change as a result. Please bear this in mind if any of the material seems inappropriate in light of subsequent events, this was clearly unavoidable.

NOTES

1. Mental Health Foundation Website, *The Social Model of Disability* https://www.mentalhealth. org.uk/learning-disabilities/a-to-z/s/social-model-disability

1

RADICALLY
INCLUSIVE LOVE

1 DISABILITY IS NOT A PUNISHMENT

> As he went along, he saw a man who had been blind from birth. His disciples asked him, 'Rabbi, who sinned, this man or his parents, that he was born blind?' Jesus replied, 'Neither he nor his parents sinned. He was born blind so that the works of God might be revealed in him'
>
> *John 9:1-3*

Before we explore how the Bible can help us to think about disability and illness, there is unfortunately one stumbling block which we must address. Tragically, some Christians believe that illness or disability may be a punishment from God, or an imperfection which makes people in some way less worthy. In support of this view they may refer to an Old Testament passage like Leviticus 21, which says that people with an infirmity are not suitable to enter the priesthood.

In the ancient world, there was little

knowledge of the causes of illness or disability, so people tried to make sense of things by attributing physical illness to sin, and mental illness to possession by evil spirits. And with very few effective treatments available people really feared becoming ill, so they often tried to stay safe by creating and maintaining a distance between themselves and members of their community who showed symptoms of mental or physical dis-ease.

As I was completing this book, the spread of the coronavirus was beginning to cause real fear and anxiety around the world. Social distancing, self-isolation, and quarantine were once again becoming an important part of our response to disease, based on scientific evidence and on public health grounds. In these circumstances it is of course essential to comply with such advice.

Pandemics like coronavirus, and the necessary social distancing and isolation that accompany them, are thankfully quite rare events in human history. But people with illnesses or disabilities have often been, and continue to be, socially isolated and excluded, not on necessary public health grounds, but due to a lack of understanding or acceptance. This makes Jesus's approach relevant to every generation. Wherever Jesus goes, people with an illness or disability are drawn to him, and he not only treats them with respect and dignity, he positively embraces them.

Reading the gospels, we can see that Jesus

must have encountered thousands of people with a complete range of physical and mental health problems. This suggests that the encounters we are told about in detail are deemed particularly significant. And what these incidents repeatedly show is that Jesus defied prevailing attitudes and conventions, to pay attention to people who had been pushed to the margins of society. In fact, we could say that the healing that Jesus offered was more than mental or physical healing, it was also social healing.

For instance, Leviticus 15:9-28 states that a woman with a discharge of blood is unclean, and that whatever she touches is polluted. But when in Luke 8:40-48 Jesus feels his clothes touched by a woman who would have been considered unclean for many years, he makes clear that he does not feel he has been in any way 'polluted' and treats her with dignity and respect, addressing her as 'My daughter'.

In the ancient world, behaviours that people found disturbing, and which we would now recognise as symptoms of a mental illness, were attributed to possession by evil spirits. People who exhibited such symptoms were feared and avoided – but every gospel has a story of Jesus healing someone who is suffering in this way. Not only does he heal them, but he tells them to return to the midst of their community and take a prominent role by sharing their story. When the Gerasene demoniac is healed, we read,

> The man from whom the demons had
> gone out asked to be allowed to stay
> with him, but he sent him away saying,
> 'Go back home and recount all that God
> has done for you.' So the man went off
> and proclaimed all over the town how
> much Jesus had done for him.
>
> *Luke 8:38-39*

This is not just the healing of an illness. This challenges the isolation, alienation and exclusion faced by so many people experiencing a mental or physical illness. The man does not simply go back into his community quietly and keep his head down, he becomes a confident and vocal member of that community.

Jesus also attracted the hostility and suspicion of the Pharisees and Herodians, by healing people on the Sabbath, deliberately making the point that compassion and concern for the welfare of others should take precedence over religious rules and tradition.

> Again he went into the synagogue, and
> there was a man present who had a
> withered hand. And they were watching
> him to see if he would cure him on the
> Sabbath day, so that they might accuse
> him. He said to the man who had the
> withered hand, 'Get up into the middle!'

> Then he said to them, 'Is it permitted on the Sabbath to do good, or to do evil; to save life, or to kill?' But they kept silence. Then he looked angrily round at them, grieved at their hardness of heart, and said to the man, 'Stretch out your hand.' He stretched it out and his hand was restored. The Pharisees went out and began at once to conspire with the Herodians against him, how to destroy him.
>
> *Mark 3:1-6*

So, we see that when Jesus encounters people who are experiencing illness or disability, what he offers them, and what he demonstrates, is a radically inclusive love. Nobody is considered unworthy, or outside the scope of social and religious inclusion, and people who were ostracised and looked down upon are treated as important and entitled to respect. In the rare circumstances where isolation is a medical necessity, this love and inclusion can be made manifest by making every effort to ensure that people who are already facing health challenges or disability receive as much support as they need.

Questions for reflection

- Do you think there are people in your community who may be excluded, not on medical advice, but consciously or unconsciously, because of an illness or disability?

- Do you sometimes feel excluded yourself? Would you feel able to discuss this with your group?

- What could be done to make your community more welcoming and inclusive?

2 HE WILL SPEAK FOR HIMSELF

His neighbours and people who had earlier seen that he was a beggar said, 'Is not this the man who used to sit and beg?' Some said, 'It is.' Others said, 'No, but he is like the man.' The man himself said, 'Yes, I am the one.' So they said to him, 'Then how were your eyes opened?' He answered, 'The man called Jesus made a paste, spread it on my eyes and said to me, "Go off and wash at Siloam." So I went and washed and could see.' They said to him, 'Where is he?' He answered, 'I do not know.'

They brought to the Pharisees the man who had been blind. It had been a Sabbath when Jesus made the paste and opened the man's eyes, so the Pharisees asked him again how he had come to see. He said to them, 'He put a paste on my eyes, and I washed, and I can see.' Then some of the Pharisees said, 'That man is not from God: he does not keep the Sabbath.' Others said, 'How can a sinner produce such signs?' And there was division among them. So they said to the blind man again, 'What have you to say about him – as it was your eyes he opened?' The man answered, 'He is a prophet.'

However, the Jews would not believe that the man had been blind and had come to see till they had sent for the parents of the man who had come to see and asked them, 'Is this man your son whom you say was born blind? If so, how can he now see?' His parents answered, 'We know that he is our son and that he was born blind, but how he can see, we do not know, nor who opened his eyes. Ask him. He is of age: he will speak for himself.' His parents said this because they were afraid of the Jews, for the Jews had already agreed that anyone who acknowledged Jesus as the Messiah should be banned from the synagogue. This was why his parents said, 'He is of age: ask him.'

So the Jews sent a second time for the man who had been blind and said to him, 'Give glory to God! We know that this man is a sinner.' He answered, 'Whether he is a sinner I don't know; one thing I do know is that though I was blind I can now see.' They said to him, 'What did he do to you? How did he open your eyes?' He replied, 'I have told you already and you did not listen. Why do you want to hear it again? Do you want to become his disciples yourselves?' At this they hurled abuse at him, 'You are his disciple, we are disciples of Moses. We know that God has spoken to Moses, but as for this man, we do not know where he comes from.' The man replied, 'The amazing thing is this: that you do not know where he comes from and he has opened my eyes! We know that God does not listen to sinners, but God does listen to someone who reveres God and does his will. Ever since the world began it is unheard of that anyone should open the eyes of someone born blind; if this man were not from God, he would not have been able to do anything.' They answered and said to him, 'You were born wholly in sin, and are you teaching us?' And they drove him out.

Jesus heard they had driven him out, and when he had found him he said, 'Do you believe in the Son of man?' He replied, 'And who is he, sir, that I may believe in him?' Jesus said to him, 'You have seen him, and he is the one speaking to you.' He said, 'Lord, I believe,' and worshipped him.

John 9:8-41

As we saw from the earlier section in John 9 at the beginning of this chapter, Jesus rejected the idea that blindness was a punishment from God for either the man born blind or his parents. Jesus heals the man's blindness, but it is what happens after this which makes it, for me, the most interesting and thought-provoking story of healing in the New Testament.

Of all the Bible stories I read in the process of writing this book, this is the one that most surprised me. What makes this one so fascinating and 'modern' for me is the character of the man born blind, and his role in the unfolding drama. He intrigued me and I thought about him a great deal – trying to imagine what he looked like, what his relationship with his parents was like, what his life was like before the story, and what it would be like afterwards, as someone who acknowledged Jesus. He is clearly not lacking in confidence or afraid to express his views – would he go on to be an evangelist, travelling like Paul and Peter, to spread the good news? Would he be persecuted, imprisoned or even executed?

The Pharisees regard the man as an inferior being. They see only someone who has come from the absolute bottom rung of society's ladder, not only disabled but destitute too, in their eyes an insignificant person of no consequence. But when they challenge him, he is more than a match for them. And when we think about the situation in which this man finds himself, his composure and presence of mind is extraordinary.

Imagine being born blind and having one's sight restored as an adult. Not restored as it would be in the present day, by a surgeon in a hospital, with an appointment for which we would probably have had plenty of time to prepare, but restored unexpectedly, by a stranger.

The shock, and sudden flood of visual stimulation would no doubt be joyous, but also overwhelming. We would need quite some time to adjust to a new and entirely different world. But instead of being given that much-needed space and time to adapt, the man faces a barrage of questions, in the first instance from his neighbours. Then he is 'brought' to the Pharisees (whether he goes willingly or not is unclear) and is subjected to some rather aggressive questioning which degenerates into abuse. Throughout, the man remains calm, articulate and poised.

And it seems clear that the man has always been like this. When his questioners, not satisfied with the man's own account of what has happened to him, send for his parents to confirm it, his parents point out that he can speak for himself, he does not need them to speak for him. This touches upon what is often a difficult issue for many people with a disability, who can be intensely frustrated and humiliated by people speaking over their heads to someone assumed to be more capable than them. It's the dreaded, 'Does he take sugar?' syndrome, where someone will ask a friend or carer the question, rather than speaking directly to the disabled person. This question has become well known as a classic example of how not to interact with disabled people. As Paul Jenkins, who has cerebral palsy, has written,

> Don't look at someone I'm with and ask if I want sugar in my tea; ask me! There is a tendency for people to treat me like I am a child, like I don't have opinions. I know many other disabled people feel like this too.[1]

We are told that when his parents say the man born blind can speak for himself, it is because they are afraid that if they acknowledge Jesus they will be banned from the synagogue. But their son proves that not only can he speak for himself, he can engage in a rather abrasive debate with confidence and a quick wit. Indeed, so much so that the Pharisees are affronted, asking indignantly, 'You were born wholly in sin, and are you teaching us?' As far as they are concerned, a man with his background should know his place, and his refusal to defer to them is considered impudent and offensive. We can almost hear the unspoken, 'How dare you?'.

When Jesus says, *'He was born blind so that the works of God might be revealed in him.'* I think the works of God were revealed in this man, as a unique and impressive individual, both as a blind man and as a sighted man. Jesus gave him sight, but the insight and intelligence were always there. In fact, the more I read this account and think about it, the more the man's importance grows, and he seems to be something of a prophet in his own right, speaking truth to power.

It is perhaps important to note that in the twenty-first century, using blindness as a metaphor for lack of perception may be offensive to people with a visual impairment. But in this scenario the man born blind is actually the most perceptive person, and the works of God are revealed in his impressive character. In his gospel John makes great use of irony, and this story is no exception – the irony in this case being that whilst the Pharisees lay claim to religious knowledge and understanding, the blind man whom Jesus heals, and whom they look down upon, is far more perceptive and insightful.

Questions for reflection

- What do you think about the man born blind? How does he strike you as a character?
- Can you imagine yourself in his position – what would it be like?
- What do you think Jesus wants us to take away from this story?

TAKING IT FURTHER

Take a look at these stories about faith healing:

The Catholic church has changed the definition of miracle in Lourdes https://www.theguardian.com/world/2006/apr/02/religion.france.

A woman with cerebral palsy attends a faith healer https://www.bbc.co.uk/bbcthree/article/12fb29da-567c-488b-8523-d1f11a79e40c

Reading these stories, do you believe healing is possible? Is it right for faith healers to try and heal a disability?

CULTURE

Under the Eye of the Clock, Christopher Nolan (Arcade Publishing, first published by St Martin's Press, 1987). Christopher Nolan was born with severe cerebral palsy that meant he was unable to speak or move outside of his wheelchair. In this excellent memoir, he describes how his family helped him overcome the limitations of his impairments and find a communication system that enabled him to write poetry and this autobiography.

Wonder, R. J. Palacio (Alfred A Knopf, 2012). The book was also made into a film starring Julia Roberts and Owen Wilson in 2017. Auggie is born with a facial disability and as a result has always been home schooled. Aged ten he is finally going to school for the first time, but will people accept him for who he is?

The Lacuna, Barbara Kingsolver (Faber and Faber, 2010). The novel follows the fortunes of Harrison Shepherd, a young man born in America but living in Mexico in the 1930s. A large part of the novel centres on his time living with Frida Kahlo and Diego Rivera, and features the challenges Kahlo faced as an artist living with disability.

Frida Kahlo. The Mexican artist frequently portrayed her disability in her self-portraits as shown in this article in the online journal *Respectability*:

https://www.respectability.org/2017/10/ frida-kahlo-self-portrait-painter-showcases-disability-art/

Disability News Service is an excellent source of news about all social, political and cultural issues pertaining to disability, with coverage often far superior to that which is found in the national media. It is edited by its founder John Pring, a disabled journalist. https://www.disabilitynewsservice.com/

No Triumph, No Tragedy. This BBC Radio 4 programme is available to listen to online, with fascinating interviews with disabled people active in all walks of life: https://www.bbc.co.uk/programmes/b00lypw4

PRAYER

God of Love,
Give us the grace to accept and value every
person,
As you enfold Creation in your all-embracing
Love.
Help us to recognise your image in the face
of everyone we meet

Without exception and with whole-hearted generosity.

NOTES

1. Alex White, *Does he take sugar with his tea?*, Scope Website, 22 October 2012 https://blog.scope.org.uk/2012/10/22/does-he-take-sugar-with-his-tea/

2

MADE IN THE IMAGE OF GOD

1 EVERYONE IS EQUAL

> God created man in the image of
>   himself,
> in the image of God he created him,
> male and female he created them.
>
> *Genesis 1:27*

This statement, that human beings were created in God's image, is the foundation of our belief that all human life is sacred, and this applies to every human being without exception. It confers upon all people an inherent and inalienable dignity and worth. I like the expression used by Quakers, that there is 'that of God in everyone'. It surely follows that all people are of equal worth, and no illness or disability can change that.

I feel that the idea we are all precious and equally important in God's eyes is expressed beautifully in Psalm 139:

O Lord, you search me and you know
    me

You yourself know my resting and my
    rising;
you discern my thoughts from afar.
You mark when I walk or lie down;
you know all my ways through and
through.

Before ever a word is on my tongue,
you know it, O Lord, through and through.
Behind and before, you besiege me,
your hand ever laid upon me.
Too wonderful for me, this knowledge;
too high, beyond my reach.

Psalm 139:1-6

I think this sense that God knows all our
imperfections and abilities, weaknesses and
strengths, is a deeply reassuring foundation on
which to build a life. What the world may see
as a flaw in our design, is in fact part of what
makes us unique.

Humanity contains endless variety. We
know that every single person ever born, and
every person yet to be born, has been and will
be, genetically unique. Disability and illness are
one manifestation of this infinite variety.

Indeed, if we look at the whole span of a
human life, categories such as disabled and

able-bodied, or ill and healthy, are seen to be shifting and fluid. Even if we are born in perfect health, very few of us will get to the end of our lives without experiencing a serious illness or acquiring a disability. Whether one is injured through an accident, develops a mental illness, or is diagnosed with a debilitating disease, we will almost all, at some stage, have to cope with a physical or mental health difficulty which makes life more of a challenge. At times we will need support and care – at times we may give support and care. We are all interdependent.

Unfortunately, rather than accepting this diversity and interdependence, human society has a tragic and enduring tendency to divide people into groups, viewing some as superior, some as inferior.

This view was taken to its extreme with terrible consequences in Nazi Germany. Hundreds of thousands of ill and disabled children and adults were systematically killed in the Aktion T-4 programme, which took its name from Tiergartenstrasse 4, the Berlin address from which the programme was coordinated.[1]

In pursuance of this policy the regime told the German population that disabled people were a burden they could not afford, 'useless eaters' and 'life unworthy of life'. Hostility and resentment were deliberately incited through propaganda, and disabled people were stripped of their humanity.[2]

One such propaganda device was a poster bearing a picture of a disabled person with a

white-coated attendant, and the text: '60,000
Reichsmarks is what this person suffering
from a hereditary disease costs the People's
community during his lifetime. Comrade, that
is your money too.'[3]

Thus, people were persuaded to see sick
and disabled people as an unaffordable and
unwanted burden. The money spent on
supporting them was, it was said, being taken
away from the poster's target audience – the
person who today would probably be described
as 'a hard-working taxpayer'.

One may think that such propaganda has
been consigned to history, but in the UK in
recent years, there has been a growing tendency
to divide people into 'workers and shirkers',
or 'strivers and scroungers', with a consequent
increase in stigma and suspicion towards people
who are not in paid work, or may be in receipt
of social security benefits. People who are
temporarily or permanently unable to do paid
work due to illness or disability can be portrayed
as not making any contribution, as a drain
on society. The tabloid press, and even senior
politicians, have circulated false and misleading
stories about disabled people and the support
they receive.[4]

This has served to erode solidarity and leave
many disabled people subject to suspicion,
abuse, and even hate crimes. As I was writing
this book, a woman taking her children to school
was abused in the street by a man who, seeing
her four-year-old daughter in a wheelchair,

shouted that she should have had an abortion because her little girl was going to be a drain on the NHS.[5] Around the same time, parents of disabled children with special educational needs were angered and upset by an article in *The Times* which was headlined, 'Pupils lose out as £400m schools funding diverted to special needs', implying that disabled children were taking resources away from those who were not disabled. After protests the headline has since been changed to 'Schools struggling to meet the costs of special needs support'.[6]

Since 2010, UK Coalition and Conservative governments have followed policies of austerity and welfare reform, which have greatly reduced the money going into our communities.[7] Drastic cuts to local authority budgets, and relentless reductions in social security support[8] have made some of the poorest people feel that they are competing for ever-diminishing resources. This can lead to resentment of disabled people and other minority groups like refugees and asylum seekers, who are perceived to be taking those resources.

As Denise Cottrell-Boyce explains in the companion Bible study guide on welcoming the stranger,[9] refugees coming to the UK are sent to the poorest areas because that is where housing is cheapest. This means that communities where people are already struggling to survive are expected to show generosity and share what little they have, while wealthier communities are untroubled by such matters. When people are facing eviction or struggling to feed their children, it is hardly surprising if some feel aggrieved when they see an asylum seeker get housed, or a disabled neighbour get what they are told by the media is 'a free car'.[10]

And sadly, this impoverishment is completely due to political choice. As Phillip Alston, the United Nations Special Rapporteur on Extreme Poverty and Human Rights reported in November 2018, after visiting the UK, 'Austerity could easily have spared the poor, if the political will had existed to do so. Resources were available to the Treasury at the last budget that could have transformed the situation of millions of people living in poverty, but the political choice was made to fund tax cuts for the wealthy instead.'[11]

The COVID-19 pandemic has also brought greatly increased anxiety for people with a disability or chronic health condition, not only because they were more at risk from the virus, but because some of government and society's responses to it left them feeling even more vulnerable.

The idea of 'herd immunity' and 'taking it on the chin' which was almost casually discussed at the beginning of the government's response, a strategy which would let the virus pass through the population with little attempt to stop it, made many disabled people feel as if they might be treated as collateral damage, their lives potentially sacrificed to protect the economy, and allow the majority to continue with minimal disruption.

On 11 March 2020, disabled journalist Frances Ryan wrote,

> Intentional or not, phrases such as 'only the long-term sick are dying' come across as somewhat flippant about – or even accepting of – the risk to millions of people with heart problems, asthma or diabetes. In a culture where ableism (prejudice against disabled people) is rife, there's a natural concern about framing a pandemic in the belief that disabled people's lives aren't as valuable as everyone else's.[12]

This concern deepened when the National Institute for Health and Care Excellence (NICE) published new guidance on the care of patients in critical care during the COVID-19 outbreak.[13] In response, Edel Harris, Chief Executive of the learning disability charity Mencap, said:

> These are unprecedented times and our NHS is under extreme pressure. But people with a learning disability and their families are deeply troubled that the latest NICE guidance for NHS intensive care doctors could result in patients with a learning disability not getting equal access to critical care and potentially dying avoidably. These guidelines suggest that those who can't do everyday tasks like cooking, managing money and personal care independently – all things that people with a learning disability

often need support with – might not get
intensive care treatment.[14]

After protests the guidelines were amended,[15]
but many disabled people were still left with the
feeling that their lives had been considered of
less value, and that the default position in much
decision-making is consciously or unconsciously,
ableist. Julie Newcombe, co-founder of Rightful
Lives and whose son Jamie has autism said: 'The
original guidance was quite simply frightening.
For a long time now, many autistic and learning
disabled people and their families have believed
that they are treated as less than human, and it
certainly felt as if the guidance was confirming
just that.'[16]

Then, emergency legislation was passed
in the form of the Coronavirus Act. Disabled
people's organisations were alarmed by some
of the provisions in the Act, one of which was
effectively to free local authorities of their duties
to provide social care support under the Care
Act 2014.[17]

A spokesperson for Disability Rights UK said:

Given the already broken social care system
this bill will almost inevitably leave many
thousands of disabled people without
essential support or any rights to request this
support. Rolling back our rights is not good
for anyone and in the current circumstances
will put many lives at risk.

Rather than removing disabled people's

right to social care support the government must treat our essential social care service as key infrastructure, alongside the NHS, and as such it must immediately provide the necessary funding to keep this vital service running.[18]

Cumulatively, this all made some disabled people feel that, whatever the government said about protecting the vulnerable, in reality their lives were less valued than the lives of others.

Another factor which could potentially put pressure on disabled people is the advances being made in genetic testing. Some disabilities, like Down's syndrome, can be detected in the womb, and in recent years such tests have become less invasive, and so less risky to the unborn child. Women who take the test and find that their baby has Down's syndrome can be given the option of going ahead with the pregnancy or having an abortion. This raises the possibility of Down's syndrome, and perhaps some other disabilities or medical conditions, eventually being eliminated from the population.

This could also mean that children born with certain disabilities would be the result of a conscious choice by the mother, to either not have the test, or decide to go ahead with a pregnancy and knowingly give birth to a disabled child. Would this element of choice change society's attitude towards such children and families?[19]

Virginia Moffatt, editor of this series, and author of the guide on approaching the end of life, spent 30 years working with and for adults with learning disabilities, including six months living in a L'Arche community. Virginia has known many people with Down's syndrome during that time. In L'Arche she lived with Philip who was a committed member of his local church and a Royal Family obsessive, and Jean, who is a talented rug maker and loves to dance. When working in a day centre she set up Corali Dance Company working with creative dancers such as Alison, Alan, Ray and Margaret who all had Down's syndrome. The company just celebrated its thirtieth birthday and still has many talented dancers with Down's syndrome among its members. Virginia believes most people with Down's syndrome can live happy lives, given the right support. However, it isn't always easy living with the condition.

Some people with Down's syndrome can be born with associated problems such as heart conditions and susceptibility to leukaemia. The grandson of a former colleague of mine (who I shall call Joe), developed a rare form of leukaemia before he was two. It required a horrendous chemotherapy regime that involved weeks in hospital. It was gruelling and painful for all of them. My colleague admits as a grandmother and mother there were times when she wished they didn't have to go through it. But despite that, Joe had a positive impact on everyone around him and when he died, people worked together to raise money for charity on his behalf. His grandmother told me that, 'Very many people remember him and have frequently commented on how knowing him has increased their knowledge and understanding of disability. What they remember is his smile and his mischief. They had the chance to know the person behind the disability.

Thinking about the implications of increased prenatal genetic testing, Virginia says,

I'm a Catholic, so I wouldn't take this genetic test or have an abortion but that is my personal choice, I couldn't expect someone else who doesn't believe that to make the same choice. I also recognise choosing to have an abortion is painful, so like euthanasia, which I discuss in my study guide,[20] the issue is very complicated.

What most concerns me in this discussion is that despite the advances of the last fifty years there is still a lot of ignorance about what it is like to live with learning disabilities, with many people believing that being disabled automatically results in a poor quality of life. Unfortunately, that ignorance can occur among health professionals, and parents often experience bad advice when discovering their child is disabled. I fear that this test means that people will have one side of the picture – and not understand that with the right support, a child with learning disabilities will flourish and become a vital part of the family and their local community. This could lead to a situation where nobody would ever choose to have a child with Down's syndrome in future, and if anyone did, that society might ostracise them and refuse to provide resources to support them. Given the pressure disabled people have been under with austerity – and the fears that some forms of euthanasia might be imposed which would put them at risk – it could lead to a society more accepting of eugenics and less accepting of difference. That's not a world I want to live in.

Virginia suggests that when couples are offered this test they should be provided with all the facts so that they make an informed choice. And that society needs to ensure there are enough resources to support parents to raise children with Down's syndrome. She concludes:

When I lived in L'Arche I lived in a house called the mustard seed based on the parable. I love the idea of the kingdom of heaven being like a small seed that grows to be an enormous tree where everyone can find rest. That's the kind of society we need to build if we want to ensure that disabled people aren't screened out and can continue to thrive.

If we believe that all people are of equal worth, then whether they are working and paying taxes should not be the only way we judge their value and contribution to society. If we value all people equally, then they must have whatever resources are required to enable them to participate in education and society on an equal footing, to fulfil their maximum potential, whatever that may be. And we should also think about what it might mean for us as a society if we screen disability out. Will the degree of difference society is prepared to accept become gradually smaller and smaller?

He also said, 'With what can we compare the kingdom of God? What parable can we find for it? It is like a mustard seed which, at the time of its sowing on the earth, is the smallest of all the seeds on earth. Yet once it is sown it grows up and becomes the biggest shrub of all and puts out big branches so that the birds of the air nest in its shade.'

Mark 4:30-32

Questions for reflection
• Have you ever witnessed or experienced abuse because of an illness or disability?

- What do you think motivated the abuse, and how do you think individuals, and society, should respond?
- If we are all made in God's image, what are the implications of ante natal screening for Christians, and for society as a whole?

2   THE LAST WILL BE FIRST

'Now the kingdom of Heaven is like a landowner going out at daybreak to hire workers for his vineyard. He made an agreement with the workers for one denarius a day and sent them to his vineyard. Going out in mid-morning he saw others standing idle in the marketplace and said to them, "You go to the vineyard too and I will give you a fair wage." So they went. At about noon and again in mid-afternoon, he went out and did the same. Then not long before sunset he went out and found more men standing around, and he said to them, "Why have you been standing here idle all day?" They said to him, "Because no one has hired us." He said to them, "You go into the vineyard too." In the evening, the owner of the vineyard said to his manager, "Call the workers and pay them their wages, starting with the last and ending with the first." So those who were hired not long before sunset came forward and received one denarius each. When the first came they expected to get more, but they too received one denarius each. They took it, but grumbled at the landowner saying, "The men who came last have done only one hour, and you have treated them the same as us, though we have done a heavy day's work in all the heat." He answered one of them and said, "My friend, I am not being unjust to you; did we not agree on one denarius? Take your earnings and go. I choose to pay the last as much as I pay you. Is it not permissible for me to do what I like with my own? Or are you envious because I am generous?" Thus the last will be first, and the first, last.'

Matthew 20:1–16

If we believe that everybody is equally precious in the eyes of God, then of course we must strive for equality. But true equality doesn't mean treating everybody the same. It means treating every person as an individual, in the way which enables them, with their different abilities and disabilities, strengths and weaknesses, to live their life to the fullest. It may be complicated in practice, but in principle it is really as simple as this instruction from Jesus:

Treat others as you would like people to treat you.

Luke 6:31

The social model of disability holds that people are often more disabled by the barriers which exist in society than by their impairment or illness. Such barriers can be physical, like inaccessible housing and public transport, or can be caused by people's attitudes, like wrongly assuming that someone with a disability is incapable of doing a certain job or activity. Recognising and removing these barriers creates progress towards equality and makes it possible for disabled people to take part in society on an equal footing.

So *steady all drooping hands and weak knees* and straighten the paths for your feet; then the injured limb will not be maimed, it will be healed instead.

Hebrews 12:12-13

However, when these physical and attitudinal barriers are combined with poverty, the suffering and social exclusion can be very acute, and in the UK, disabled people are more likely to be living in poverty than the general population. A report commissioned by the Joseph Rowntree Foundation in 2016 found that 44 per cent of disabled young adults are in poverty, and two-thirds of single disabled people living alone are in poverty.[21]

When considering these issues, I have found the parable of the workers in the vineyard, cited above, very significant.

In his book *The Upside-Down Bible*,[22] Symon Hill shared a selection of passages with groups of people who were not familiar with the Bible or traditional interpretations of the passages they read. Their responses to this parable of the labourers in the vineyard varied greatly. Some readers were angry with the landowner and saw him as a bad employer, whilst others felt that the situation described was in fact quite a desirable one.

One of the readers, Samantha, said:

> I would have to identify with the late arrivals. As a person with a disability, I have often had to claim benefits because of being unable to keep up with normal 'hardworking' people.[23]

Pointing out that in the parable, at the end of the day everyone got what they needed to live on, she felt that the parable is about social justice, saying:

> I think the point Jesus is making is that to resent others receiving the same financial support, comfort and – ultimately – respect as you, and to consider them to deserve less

of these things than you, is not a loving attitude towards others.

Jesus says at the beginning of the parable that this is what the Kingdom of Heaven is like – everyone gets what they need to live, with no exceptions made. Those who did not work a full day, for whatever reason, were not deprived of what they needed.

It is perfectly possible to create a society like this, where everybody receives what they need to live a decent life, regardless of what they are able to contribute in terms of paid employment.

In Catholic Social Teaching, the principle of 'the universal destination of goods' means that, as God created the earth for all mankind, then all mankind is entitled to a share in the wealth of the earth.[24] As Pope Pius XI wrote in 1931:

> To each, therefore, must be given his own share of goods, and the distribution of created goods, which, as every discerning person knows, is labouring today under the gravest evils due to the huge disparity between the few exceedingly rich and the unnumbered propertyless, must be effectively called back to and brought into conformity with the norms of the common good, that is, social justice.
>
> *Quadragesimo Anno* para 58[25]

Unfortunately, over the last decade or so in the UK, the policies of successive Coalition and Conservative governments have taken us further and further away from a just or supportive model of society, particularly where ill and disabled people and carers are concerned. Since 2010, drastic cuts to public spending, particularly the funding of local authorities, has meant that many services which disabled people of all ages rely on, like social care, are simply not available to all who need them.

The Welfare Reform Act 2012 also introduced numerous measures which had a disproportionate impact on disabled people, like the bedroom tax, which reduced the already meagre incomes of many who were ill or disabled. Disability Living Allowance was abolished and replaced with the Personal Independence Payment, which has different eligibility criteria and has resulted in around 650,000 people having their support cut or removed altogether. Assessments for disability benefits have produced notoriously bad outcomes, with medically unqualified Decision Makers in the Department for Work and Pensions able to disregard the opinion of a claimant's GP or consultant and declare them fit to work, or not in need of support. More than one academic study has found that these assessments are causing permanent damage to the mental health of some claimants.[26]

But perhaps the harshest and most unreasonable welfare reform measure was the extension of benefit sanctions to people who are unfit to work. It is important to understand that sanctions are not imposed for benefit fraud – that is an entirely different matter and is dealt with through the criminal justice system. Sanctions are applied if a claimant is deemed not to have fulfilled the conditions of their claimant commitment – for example by being late for a meeting at the Jobcentre, missing a phone call, or not applying for a specific number of jobs in a week.

A sanction means a person's benefit is reduced or stopped, leaving them with an extremely low income – or no income at all. In 2012 this sanctions regime was extended to people who were officially acknowledged to be unfit to work, but were required to undertake 'work related activity', like updating their CV or attending a course or interviews at the Jobcentre. The people who are most ill and have the most difficult lives will naturally find it most difficult to comply with these requirements, and so are most likely to be sanctioned.

In 2015 a group of churches published a research report, *Time To Rethink Benefit Sanctions*, in which they found that 100 people with severe mental illness were being sanctioned each day. Paul Morrison, Public Issues Policy Adviser for the Methodist Church, said: 'Sanctioning someone with a mental health problem for being late for a meeting is like sanctioning someone with a broken leg for limping. The fact that this system punishes people for the symptoms of their illness is a clear and worrying sign that it is fundamentally flawed,'[27] Five years later, in January 2020, Conservative government ministers were still refusing to even conduct an assessment of the impact of sanctions on mental health.[28]

The flagship policy of welfare reform, Universal Credit, appeared to have been designed with very little consideration for the needs of ill or disabled people. In 2012 Citizens Advice published a report *Disability and Universal Credit*, in which Baroness Tanni Grey-Thompson wrote, 'Under the new system, financial support for some groups of disabled people will be much lower than current support available for people in the same circumstances. Cuts such as those to support for most disabled children and disabled adults living alone are going to make the future considerably bleaker for many of the most vulnerable households in Britain.'[29]

These government policies and their impact on disabled people have not gone unnoticed on the international stage. In 2016 the United Nations Committee on the Rights of Persons with Disabilities ruled that the UK government had committed 'grave and systematic' violations of the human rights of disabled people in the UK, leading to 'a human catastrophe'.[30] In the report of his 2018 visit to the UK mentioned above, Professor Philip Alston, the UN Special Rapporteur on Extreme Poverty and Human Rights, investigated the UK and said that 'great misery' had been 'inflicted unnecessarily'. He concluded:

British compassion for those who are suffering has been replaced by a punitive, mean-spirited, and often callous approach apparently designed to instil discipline where it is least useful, to impose a rigid order on the lives of those least capable of coping with today's world, and elevating the goal of enforcing blind compliance over a genuine concern to improve the well-being of those at the lowest levels of British society.[31]

One of the manifestations of this removal of support for disabled people is now seen at foodbanks around the country. In *The State of Hunger 2019*, an independent research report conducted by Heriot-Watt University and commissioned by the Trussell Trust, it was reported that almost three-quarters of people at food banks live in households affected by ill-health or disability, and 94 per cent of foodbank users are destitute. The average weekly income for a household referred to a foodbank, after housing costs, is £50.[32] There has also been a steep rise in homelessness amongst people who are ill and disabled, with the shocking sight of wheelchair users living on the streets, something I never imagined would happen in the UK.[33]

Jesus repeatedly takes society's values and conventions and turns them on their head. The first will be last and the last will be first, the 'unclean' will be touched, people will be healed on the Sabbath, the excluded will be brought back into the centre. This echoes those revolutionary lines in the Magnificat:

> He has exerted the power of his arm,
> he has scattered the proud in the thoughts of their heart.
> He has taken down princes from thrones and raised up the lowly.
> He has filled the hungry with good things, and sent the rich away empty.
>
> *Luke 1:51-55*

By following Jesus's example of radically inclusive love, we can strive to create a society in which all people can live their lives to the fullest. This is not just a question of attitudes, but one of resources, and perhaps most importantly where human dignity is concerned, incomes. When Neil Carpenter became an advocate for people with a learning disability in Cornwall, he said, 'When I began work as a volunteer, one of my strongest impressions as I went to different day centres or visited people at home was how poor almost everyone seemed, as if poverty was an inevitable part of having a learning disability.'

The gospels are quite clear that the 'thoughts and prayers' approach to such inequality and injustice is simply not adequate, what is required is concrete action.

> If one of the brothers or one of the sisters is in need of clothes and has not enough food to live on, and one of you says to them, 'Go in peace. Keep warm and eat plenty,' without giving them the bare necessities of life, what good is that? In the same way faith: if good deeds do not go with it, it is quite dead by itself.
>
> *James 2:15-18*

As a Christian community we clearly have a moral responsibility to ensure that disability or illness is not a route to poverty and destitution, but in too many cases we are currently failing in that. Many Christians have responded admirably to increased homelessness and hunger by volunteering and donating to charities like foodbanks and night shelters, but this deals with the symptoms of poverty, rather than eliminating poverty itself.

Justice requires that we question the policies and values which have helped to create this poverty and demand the changes necessary to make society fairer. As Nelson Mandela said in Trafalgar Square in 2005:

Like slavery and apartheid, poverty is not natural. It is man-made and it can be overcome and eradicated by the actions of human beings. And overcoming poverty is not a gesture of charity. It is an act of justice. It is the protection of a fundamental human right, the right to dignity and a decent life.[34]

It is certainly not beyond our wit or our resources to ensure that everybody is able to lead a dignified and decent life. The arrival of the coronavirus, COVID-19, has dramatically highlighted how financially precarious are the lives of many people in the UK now, particularly those in low paid, insecure work who have no savings. With many more people encountering the benefits system for perhaps the first time, or the first time in many years, they are realising how mean and inadequate it has become. Media commentators who have previously portrayed living on benefits as a comfortable and easy lifestyle choice are now aghast that people could be expected to live on so little, even for a few months. This has resulted in more interest in alternative systems, such as a Universal Basic Income.

The Centre for Welfare Reform, led by Dr Simon Duffy, strongly supports a Basic Income, and has gone further, to propose a Basic Income Plus, which would take into account the different needs of disabled people and carers. Dr Duffy writes that

> it is a good way to protect the human rights of disabled people, which includes the need for an adequate and secure income, with no stigma and with no penalties for working, saving or contributing in other ways' [35]

The impact of the coronavirus has undoubtedly demonstrated the need for some form of simple and guaranteed security for all of us, to reduce stress, anxiety and hardship for individuals, and to make society more resilient in any future crisis

TAKING IT FURTHER

If you don't currently have a disability or significant health problem: imagine you are seriously injured in an accident, or are diagnosed with a serious illness. Would you lose your job? If you became a wheelchair user, would your home be suitable, or would you need to make significant adaptations, or even move? Undertake some research into what financial and practical help would be available for you, and how easy this is to access.

If you are disabled: think about any changes in your community that could improve your quality of life, discuss them with the group, and share your ideas with local councillors or your Member of Parliament

CULTURE

Crippled: Austerity and the demonisation of disabled people. Dr Frances Ryan is a disabled writer working for the *Guardian* newspaper. Her book documents how recent political policies have had a devastating impact on the lives of disabled people in the UK.

Austerity's Victims: Living with a learning disability under Cameron and May, Neil Carpenter. The book concentrates on five men with a learning disability, giving an insight into their lives. It details their struggles with the system of assessments and applications they are forced to go through to obtain a meagre income, and we see how their quality of life deteriorates as the support they are given shrinks.

I, Daniel Blake is a film directed by Ken Loach. It tells the story of a middle-aged man recovering from a heart attack, his struggle to survive while unable to work, and his experience of trying to navigate the system which is supposed to support him.

Nothing More and Nothing Less by Virginia Moffatt is a Lent study guide that uses *I, Daniel Blake* as a basis to discuss oppression and suffering.

A World Without Down's Syndrome. Actor and writer Sally Phillips has a son with Down's syndrome. She made a documentary for the BBC, *A World Without Down's Syndrome?* about the implications of non-invasive pre-natal screening tests for Down's Syndrome. Clips of the programme are available on the BBC website https://www.bbc.co.uk/programmes/b07ycbj5

Awkward Beauty. Leading British colourist Lucy Jones was born with cerebral palsy and describes herself as 'wobbly'. She has painted a variety of subjects, including a series of self-portraits which feature her mobility aids, published in this book. She often paints in a kneeling position, because 'it's less far to fall'.

The Corali Dance Company is based at the Ovalhouse Theatre in London. It has been producing critically acclaimed shows performed by adults with learning disabilities for 30 years.

PRAYER

God of Justice,

Help us to build a society in which all people can feel at home,

In which all people can flourish and live life in all its fullness.

Give us the courage to speak truth to power,

And the persistence to continue until your justice prevails.

NOTES

1. Holocaust Memorial Day Trust Website, *Disabled People*: https://www.hmd.org.uk/learn-about-the-holocaust-and-genocides/nazi-persecution/disabled-people/

2. Olga Khazan, 'Remembering the Nazis disabled victims', *The Atlantic*, 3 September 2014: https://www.theatlantic.com/health/archive/2014/09/a-memorial-to-the-nazis-disabled-victims/379528/

3. Nazi poster: https://www.warhistoryonline.com/world-war-ii/action-t4-nazi-euthanasia-programme.html

4. John Pring, 'Tory boss 'rebuked' over party's latest misuse of benefit figures', *Disability News Service*, 31 May 2013: https://www.disabilitynewsservice.com/tory-boss-rebuked-over-partys-latest-misuse-of-benefit-figures)/

5. Sophia Douro, 'Girl 4 in a wheelchair told she's 'a drain on society' and shouldn't be alive', *Metro*, 24 October 2019: https://metro.co.uk/2019/10/24/girl-4-in-wheelchair-told-shes-a-drain-on-society-and-shouldnt-be-alive-10975552/

6. Greg Hurst, 'Schools 'struggling to meet the cost of special needs support', *The Times*, 14 October 2019.

7. Nicholas Watt, 'Local government cuts hitting poorest areas hardest, figures show', *Guardian*, 30 January 2014: https://www.theguardian.com/society/2014/jan/30/local-government-cuts-poorest-areas

8. Patrick Butler, 'Welfare spending for UK's poorest shrinks by £37 billion', *Guardian*, 23 September 2018: https://www.theguardian.com/politics/2018/sep/23/welfare-spending-uk-poorest-austerity-frank-field

9. Denise Cottrell-Boyce, *How The Bible Can Help Us Understand Welcoming the Stranger* (Darton, Longman and Todd, 2020)

10. Peter Walker, 'Benefit cuts are fuelling abuse of disabled people, say charities', *Guardian*, 5 February 2012: https://www.theguardian.com/society/2012/feb/05/benefit-cuts-fuelling-abuse-disabled-people

11. Professor Philip Alston, *Statement on Visit to the United Kingdom* by Professor Philip Alston United

Nations Special Rapporteur on extreme poverty and human rights, United Nations, Human Rights Office of the High Commissioner, 16 November 2018

12. Frances Ryan, 'Coronavirus hits ill and disabled people hardest, so why is society writing us off?', *Guardian*, 11 March 2020 https://www.theguardian.com/commentisfree/2020/mar/11/coronavirus-ill-disabled-people (Mencap press release)

13. NICE. *Nice publishes first rapid COVID-19 guidelines*, 21 March 2020: https://www.nice.org.uk/news/article/nice-publishes-first-rapid-covid-19-guidelines

14. Ed Harris, *Mencap responds to 'deeply troubling' NICE new Covid-19 advice guidance'*, 20 March 2020: https://www.mencap.org.uk/press-release/mencap-responds-deeply-troubling-new-nice-covid-19-guidance.

15. Zoe Kleinman. *Coronavirus 'frailty score' angers special needs parents*. BBC website 26 March 2020. https://www.bbc.co.uk/news/health-52022965

16. Shaun Lintern, 'Coronavirus: U turn on critical care advice for NHS amid fears disabled people will be denied treatment', *Independent*, 25 March 2020.

17. UK Parliament, *Coronavirus bill*. 17 March 2020: https://services.parliament.uk/Bills/2019-21/coronavirus.htm

18. Lucas Comiskey, 'Coronavirus bill: Disabled people in Islington fear they'll be "thrown under a bus" if care act is suspended', *Islington Gazette*, 24 March 2020: https://services.parliament.uk/Bills/2019-21/coronavirus.htm

19. Viv Groskop, 'Sally Phillips, do we really want a world without Down's Syndrome?' *Guardian*, 1 October 2016: https://www.theguardian.com/lifeandstyle/2016/oct/01/do-we-really-want-a-world-without-downs-syndrome-ds-prenatal-test

20. Virginia Moffatt. *How The Bible Can Help Us Understand Approaching the End of Life* (Darton, Longman and Todd, 2020).

21. Adam Tinson, Hannah Aldridge, Theo Barry Born, Ceri Hughes, *Disability and Poverty*, NPI, August 2016: https://www.npi.org.uk/publications/income-and-poverty/disability-and-poverty/

22. Symon Hill, *The Upside-Down Bible* (Darton, Longman and Todd, 2016)

23. *Ibid*.

24. Catechism of the Catholic Church, *Catholic social teaching*, Paragraph 2403

25. Pius X1 *Quadragesimo Anno* (Libere Editrice Vaticana, 15 May1931)

26. Jon Stone, 'DWP's fit-to-work tests "cause permanent damage to mental health"', *Independent* 13 March 2017: https://www.independent.co.uk/news/uk/politics/fit-to-work-wca-tests-mental-health-dwp-work-capability-assessment-benefits-esa-pip-a7623686.html

27. Joint Public Issues Team, *Time to rethink sanctions* (Methodist Publishing, 2015): http://www.jointpublicissues.org.uk/wp-content/uploads/Time-to-Rethink-Sanctions-Report.pdf

28. May Bulman, 'Ministers refuse to assess impact of benefits sanctions on mental health despite warnings of links to suicides', *Independent*, 25

January 2020: https://www.independent.co.uk/news/uk/politics/benefit-sanctions-mental-health-dwp-universal-credit-a9301691.html

29. Sue Royston, *Universal Credit*, Citizens Advice, 2012: https://www.citizensadvice.org.uk/about-us/policy/policy-research-topics/welfare-policy-research-surveys-and-consultation-responses/welfare-policy-research/disability-and-universal-credit/

30. John Pring, 'UN confirms that UK government's treaty violations were both grave AND systematic', *Disability News Service*, 29 June 2017: https://www.disabilitynewsservice.com/un-confirms-that-uk-governments-treaty-violations-were-both-grave-and-systematic/

31. Professor Philip Alston, *Statement on Visit to the United Kingdom* by Professor Philip Alston, United Nations Special Rapporteur, on extreme poverty and human rights, United Nations, Human Rights Office of the High Commissioner, 16 November 2018: https://www.ohchr.org/Documents/Issues/Poverty/EOM_GB_16Nov2018.pdf

32. Filip Sosenko, Mandy Littlewood, Glen Bramley, Suzanne Fitzpatrick, Janice Blenkinsopp, Jenny Wood, *State Of Hunger. A Study of Poverty and Food Insecurity in the UK*, November 2019, The Trussell Trust: https://www.stateofhunger.org/

33. May Bulman, 'Homelessness among ill and disabled people rises 53% in a year, figures show', *Independent*, 18 December 2019: https://www.crisis.org.uk/about-us/media-centre/number-of-people-with-physical-ill-health-or-disability-experiencing-homelessness-rises-by-53-crisis-response/

34. BBC News website, *In full: Mandela's poverty speech*, 3 February 2005: http://news.bbc.co.uk/1/hi/uk_politics/4232603.stm

35. Simon Duffy, *Basic income plus*, The Centre for Welfare Reform, 2016: https://centreforwelfarereform.org/library/basic-income-plus.html

3

STRENGTH, WEAKNESS AND THE AUTHORITY OF SUFFERING

1 STRENGTH IN WEAKNESS, WEAKNESS IN STRENGTH

> While the Jews demand signs and the Greeks seek wisdom, we are proclaiming a crucified Christ: to the Jews a stumbling-block, to the gentiles foolishness, but to those who have been called, both Jews and Greeks, a Christ who is both the power of God and the wisdom of God. God's folly is wiser than human wisdom, and God's weakness is stronger than human strength. Brothers and sisters, consider your own call; not many of you are wise by human standards, not many influential, not many of noble birth. No, God chose the foolish things of the world to shame the wise; God chose the weak things of the world to shame the strong.
>
> *1 Corinthians 1:22-27*

When I began writing this section of the book, the provisional title was 'strength in weakness'. But the more I read the gospels and thought about these two concepts, the more I felt that they were often interchangeable, and very much dependent on context and perspective. How do we decide to categorise a person as 'weak, but showing strength' or 'strong, but with a weakness'? Aren't we all a mixture of both weakness and strength?

In the eyes of the world, the crucifixion looked like folly and failure. In the eyes of the world, a crucified Christ appeared weak and defeated. But the world's values are not God's values. In God's eyes, and for God's purposes, what is seen as weakness can be strength, and those who appear strong and successful may in fact be vulnerable and living in a way that does not satisfy them or nourish their souls.

One of the most influential people in the world today is the young environmental activist Greta Thunberg. As a schoolgirl, Thunberg had absolutely no power to force anybody to do anything, but through her example she has caused millions of people around the world to protest about climate change, quickly propelling the issue to the top of the political agenda.

When she first began her school strike for the climate in 2018, Thunberg sat alone every Friday on the pavement outside the Swedish parliament building. As a 15-year-old girl who was quite small for her age, with a homemade placard, she looked fragile and insignificant. No doubt many people who saw early reports of her protest viewed it as futile, a waste of time. How was a single schoolgirl going to make a difference to anything? As we now know, those people could not have been more wrong.

Yet not only did Greta Thunberg act from a position of powerlessness, she also has what the world would class as a disability – autism. But she refers to autism as her superpower, saying,

> Being different is a gift. It makes me see things from outside the box. I don't easily fall for lies, I can see through things. If I would've been like everyone else, I wouldn't have started this school strike for instance.[1]

When we consider the impact of Thunberg's example on people much older and more powerful than herself, forcing them to reconsider their priorities, we can see that perhaps our ideas about weakness and strength are too narrow and restrictive. And Christianity is built on the life of someone who was, in the eyes of much of the world, a failure. Something that followers like Paul also understood.

> About this, I three times pleaded with the Lord that it might leave me, but he answered me, 'My grace is enough for you: for power is at the full in weakness.' So I am happy to boast about my weaknesses so that the power of Christ

> may dwell in me; therefore I am content with weaknesses, insults, constraints, persecutions and distress for Christ's sake. For whenever I am weak, then am I strong.
>
> *2 Corinthians 12:7-10*

Paul is very open about the fact that he himself has a weakness or illness, which he refers to several times. Even with this perceived weakness, Paul went on to become one of the most important figures in Christianity, and so arguably in human history. For Christians, the crucifixion of Jesus has redefined suffering, and the early Christian community, far from rejecting Paul because of his weakness or illness, treated him with respect and recognised his authority as God's messenger. Indeed, Paul frequently refers to his afflictions as the sign of his authority.

> Brothers and sisters, I beg you, become like me, as I have become like you. You have done me no wrong; but you know that it was through a sickness of the flesh that I first proclaimed to you the gospel, yet though my illness was a trial to you, you did not despise me or insult me; instead, you welcomed me as a messenger of God, as Christ Jesus.
>
> *Galatians 4:12-14*

I was given a striking example of how people who appear weak can be a source of strength to others at my mother's funeral. After the Mass, a person whom I'd never met offered their condolences, and I was slightly at a loss to know what their connection had been to my Mum. When I asked, they replied, 'Oh, your Mum got me through my cancer.'

They explained that though Mum had never met them she knew their family, and had heard about the cancer diagnosis that way. Although at the time Mum was quite frail, virtually housebound and often bedbound, she phoned to wish them well as they began their treatment. They enjoyed their chat, and after that she phoned on a regular basis, as they struggled with the gruelling side effects. She occasionally sent little cards and encouraging messages, and they knew she was praying for them. This support, they said, had played a huge role in their recovery.

To the world, my elderly Mum may have appeared weak and dependent on the care of others, but her concern and compassion for a person much younger than herself had helped carry them through the biggest challenge of their life. Strength can come in all shapes and sizes, and is not the sole preserve of the fit and healthy. As Paul says,

> There are varieties of gifts, but the same Spirit; and there are varieties of services, but the same Lord. There are varieties of activities, but the same God who activates all of them in everyone. To each person the manifestation of the Spirit is given for the general good.'
>
> *1 Corinthians 12:4-8*

Kintsugi (golden joinery), or Kintsukuroi (golden repair) is the Japanese art of repairing broken pottery using lacquer mixed with powdered gold, silver, or platinum. Thus, a broken object is not rejected but is repaired and becomes more highly prized. The breakage and repair become part of the history of an object, which enhance its beauty and value, rather than being something to be concealed.

This technique extends into a philosophy of life, which says that we are all fragile, but that should not prevent us from living our lives to the full. We should not live in fear of being broken, and when it happens, as it surely will, we should not conceal the pain and grief we have experienced. We shouldn't sweep our brokenness away like pieces of broken crockery, but acknowledge the damage and put ourselves back together as well as we can. Just like the shimmering joins of a kintsugi object, the scars we carry afterwards, whether physical or emotional, signify the challenges we have overcome, and make us wiser, more substantial people.

In his song 'Anthem', Leonard Cohen expresses his belief that what may appear to be a weakness or an imperfection is actually the thing that opens us up to enlightenment and wisdom. He suggests that we should not worry about whether what we offer is perfect, because it is through the cracks that light gets in.

It is a cliché to regard suffering as source of creativity, the artist suffering for his art, but it is very striking to learn how many of the world's most famous artists experienced some form of illness or disability, and how much of an influence that may have been on the work they produced.

Henri Matisse, for instance, had no interest in art until he became ill and spent a year in bed when he was 20. His mother bought him a box of paints to help pass the time, and he discovered a passion for painting. Eventually he became the internationally renowned leader of the Fauvist movement. In his seventies, after surgery for cancer, Matisse was bedridden again, and then became a wheelchair user. During these last 14 years of his life, which he described as *'une seconde vie'* he developed a completely new style of art. He said that his experience of illness and disability made him rethink his priorities, and he felt more free to express himself. In his final project he designed every aspect of the décor for a Dominican chapel in Vence, France.

However, we should also be careful not to

celebrate perceived weakness or vulnerability in a way which has been dubbed 'inspiration porn'. Disabled people who may be struggling with the basics of day to day life can find it patronising and intensely irritating to have themselves, or other disabled people, held up as inspirational. For example, when the 2012 Paralympics were held in London, Channel 4 branded its coverage of the event *The Superhumans*. At a time when government policies of welfare reform and austerity were beginning to make life extremely difficult for many disabled people, particularly those living in poverty, the idea that they should be aiming to achieve extraordinary things as an inspiration to others was not welcome. The reflected glory of an Olympic medal was no substitute for respect and fair treatment. This point was underlined by the fact that, even as Paralympic athletes were being lauded as inspirational examples, government policies would cause some to lose the adapted vehicles which allowed them to get to training sessions.[2]

So, the more we think about strength and weakness, the more it becomes clear that when we classify people as possessing either characteristic, it can be rather inaccurate. In reality, those who appear to have a weakness may be strong, and those who appear strong may in fact be suffering due to unseen vulnerabilities. But as we will see in the next section, people who go through suffering can acquire a wisdom which gives them a hard-earned and genuine authority.

Questions for reflection

- Do you know someone who has suffered, but has been a source of strength to you or others?
- Do you know someone who to the world may appear weak but who does in fact have great strength?
- Do you think people see you as weak, or strong? Why? Does it matter?

2 THE AUTHORITY OF SUFFERING

'Thomas, called the Twin, who was one of the Twelve, was not with them when Jesus came. So the other disciples said to him, 'We have seen the Lord,' but he answered, 'Unless I see in his hands the mark of the nails and put my finger in the mark of the nails, and my hand into his side, I will not believe.' Eight days later the disciples were in the house again and Thomas was with them. Although the doors were closed, Jesus came and stood among them and said, 'Peace be with you.' Then he said to Thomas, 'Put your finger here, and see my hands. Reach out your hand and put it in my side. Do not doubt but believe.' Thomas replied, 'My Lord and my God!''

John 20:24-29

When Thomas wanted proof that Jesus was who he said he was, he did not ask Jesus to perform a miracle and show his power. It was the marks of suffering which Thomas accepted as proof of Jesus's authenticity, and thus his authority. In our ordinary lives we too can find that when people have been through suffering it makes them more qualified to speak on certain subjects, and so in a sense gives them more authority.

Bill Braviner is a vicar in the Church of England who has struggled with significant anxiety and depression. In a book he co-authored, *Pilgrims in the Dark*, he writes that one of the things which helped him when he was at a very low point in his life was watching the film *The Passion of the Christ*.

One Easter Saturday, when he was too ill to attend a church service, Bill took the DVD down from the shelf and started to watch. He found himself weeping as he saw Jesus being rejected and mocked, feeling a profound sense of connection with his suffering. Then, in the brief resurrection scene, he saw, and really appreciated for the first time, that the risen Jesus still bore his wounds. Something began to change for him, and over a period of weeks he continued to think about the film.

Bill writes:

I knew that watching *The Passion of the Christ* had been significant, and that there was something profound in that very short resurrection scene. It was when I was reading some of the gospel passages about Jesus'

resurrection appearances that realisation
dawned regarding what was so significant:
it was that Jesus was risen with his wounds.
To be wounded, damaged, scarred, beaten
up by life – these were things Jesus took
into his resurrection, into the heart of God.
Suddenly, something in my heart and head
went 'bang!' and I realised I was acceptable.
I realised that this great failing of mine, this
crumbling and falling and woundedness, this
anxiety and depression and mental dis-ease,
this was all stuff that Jesus had wrapped
up into that resurrection, and I needn't
be ashamed of these wounds, or fearful of
them. I could bear them in resurrection life.
That was profoundly healing.[3]

Bill remains a vicar and is now disability officer
for Durham diocese. Together with two friends
he went on to found the group 'Disability and
Jesus', which aims to ensure that people with
an illness or disability are not only accepted or
included in the church but are welcomed into
positions of influence and leadership. Their
motto is 'A church without disabled people is
a disabled church' as they feel strongly that the
churches are currently missing out on the gifts
of many people with experience of illness and
disability. The other co-founders of the group
are Dave Lucas, an access auditor and low-vision
awareness trainer who is himself blind, and
Katie Tupling, who has cerebral palsy, is vicar of

two parishes in the Sheffield Diocese and is also the diocesan disability officer. Bill, Dave and Katie can speak with authority on matters of disability, because of their experience.

When this authority is disregarded or simply overlooked, preventable problems inevitably occur. For instance, when the design for a new memorial to the Peterloo Massacre was unveiled in Manchester, wheelchair users and others with mobility problems were shocked. The design was of a mound or hill with concentric steps, which people can walk up to a flat top. The intention was that it would be a communal space, people could climb, stand, and sit on it together. But that would not be possible for many disabled people, as there was no disabled access. A monument to people who had suffered and died struggling for democracy and basic rights had been designed in a way that excluded a section of the population which is still struggling for equality. Immediately there were protests, the designer was sincerely apologetic and promised a redesign. But how much better could it have been if disabled people had been consulted from the start? If the designers had tapped into the authority of disabled people, the problem could have been avoided. And of course, while this was a highly symbolic project, it was not going to have a major impact on anyone's quality of life. When housing, public buildings and transport infrastructure are designed without the authoritative input of disabled people, the results can be seriously detrimental.

The word authority is linked to the word author, and we could say that experience authors us, in the sense that everything we live through changes us and teaches us something. This is widely understood and acknowledged in common expressions like, 'Been there, got the t-shirt'. So, when we speak about things of which we have real experience, our words carry weight. When the experience we speak from is one of suffering, then it is seen as hard-earned, and so may be even more valued.

Part of our culture that represents this authority of suffering to me is the poetry of the First World War. Poets like Siegfried Sassoon, who was wounded and later admitted to a psychiatric hospital, unflinchingly wrote about the obscene reality of what he had seen and felt on the battlefield. The public reacted strongly, and even some of his friends said his poems were too graphic. But nobody could question their authenticity, or the moral authority with which Sassoon could speak about such things.

In the present day, Veterans for Peace are men and women who have served in the Armed Forces and through their experience have decided that, although they still believe in a right to self-defence, 'war is not the solution to the problems we face in the twenty-first century'.

When Jill Segger, a Quaker peace campaigner, reviewed the film *War School* in which a number of these veterans appear, she wrote:

They carry themselves tightly. They are troubled men. Across a forty-year age range, we see them remembering not only the physical horrors they have seen, but the recollection of promises broken, of civilians traumatised and betrayed. Their own dawning awareness of the part they had been moulded to play is never going to leave them.

For me, the most harrowing among these was the youngest veteran. Wayne Sharrocks began his army training as a minor, joining up on his seventeenth birthday, and was later deployed to Afghanistan where he was injured in a bomb blast. His experiences, both of training and combat, were described with an anxious smile that came quickly and departed just as suddenly, bearing no relation to the context of his narrative, and accompanied by an occasional nervous laugh which was more a punctuation of distress than any expression of amusement or irony. The camera lingered on his damaged young face when he had run out of words. In most films, this kind of uncomfortable footage is discarded in the edit suite. Here, mercilessly, it revealed the return of an unforgettably haunted expression.[4]

When these veterans campaign for peace, people may disagree with them, but they can never be dismissed as unpatriotic, or cowardly. They carry the authority of their suffering.

This authority of suffering is often employed in a therapeutic way. The term 'wounded healer' was coined by psychologist Carl Jung, but the idea goes back to Greek mythology, when the centaur Chiron was injured by a poisoned arrow fired by Hercules. Chiron was in great pain for the rest of his life, but became a legendary healer.

In this spirit of the wounded healer, people recovering from addictions can become mentors to those at an earlier stage on their journey. More than any healthcare professional or therapist, they can understand the struggles and challenges an addict is going through, and the person they are mentoring will often value their advice, and respect their opinion more, because they know that the person is speaking from their own difficult experience. A good example of this is Alcoholics Anonymous, 'a fellowship of men and women who share their experience, strength and hope with each other that they may solve their common problem and help others to recover from alcoholism'. The value of lived experience is also starting to be recognised in the NHS, where patients can be designated 'experts by experience' and involved in consultations and discussions.

So, what the world sees as weakness may not in fact be weakness at all, but a different kind of strength, which provides another way of seeing or another path to take. As for suffering, whilst it is right and natural to wish to avoid it if at all possible, when we have endured it, it can give us insights and understanding which enable us to help others, and the ability to speak with greater authority.

Questions for reflection

- Have you had an experience of suffering which you feel has given you some ability to help or understand others?
- Have you ever met someone whose suffering has challenged your thinking?
- How do you think we can enhance the authority of those who suffer to talk about things that matter?

TAKING IT FURTHER

Christopher Reeve was an actor made famous by the *Superman* movies in the 1980s till an accident resulted in him becoming seriously physically disabled.

Take a look at this YouTube compilation of Reeve as Superman:

https://www.youtube.com/watch?v=BF8Tc-7i9dw

Now watch some of these interviews with him after his accident:

https://www.christopherreeve.org/about-us/christopher-and-dana/christopher-reeve-interview

What has Reeve's experience got to teach us about weakness and strength? Watching these videos do you feel sorry for him/humbled by him/or a mixture of both?

CULTURE

Kintsugi objects are a powerful reminder that there is beauty in brokenness. You can find some examples on this website:

https://www.lifegate.com/people/lifestyle/kintsugi

The Resurrection **by Charles Murray (1944) and by Otto Dix (1949)** Consider the different emotions in these two paintings of the same subject, and think about how they may reflect the mood of the times in which they were painted.

Greta Thunberg's TED Talk. In this talk, the climate activist discusses how she started the school strike and how her autism is a key part of her successful campaigning: https://www.ted.com/talks/greta_thunberg_school_strike_for_climate_save_the_world_by_changing_the_rules/transcript

The Penguin Book of First World War Poets. A classic collection of poems by men whose lives and poetry would have been quite different if they had not had to go to war.

'Anthem'. A song by Leonard Cohen.

PRAYER

God of Hope,
When we are weak and struggling help us to
be strong,

And when we are strong and confident help
us to be compassionate.
Help us to use all our gifts and experiences
To show your love to the world.

NOTES

1. Ian Birrell, 'Greta Thunberg teaches us about autism as much as climate change' *Guardian* 23 April 2019: https://www.theguardian.com/commentisfree/2019/apr/23/greta-thunberg-autism

2. John Pring, 'The government has stripped Paralympians of their motability vehicles', *Disability News Service*, 25 August 2016. https://www.disabilitynewsservice.com/government-has-stripped-paralympians-of-their-motability-vehicles/

3. Katie Tupling, Dave Lucas and Bill Braviner, *Pilgrims in the Dark*, Disability and Jesus website, *2018:* http://disabilityandjesus.org.uk/

4. Jill Segger, *War and the imagining of alternatives: some questions for politicians*, 20 November 2019, http://www.ekklesia.co.uk/node/29088

4

SUFFERING

1 THE DARKNESS OF SUFFERING

> Since in Jesus, the Son of God, we have
> the supreme high priest who has gone
> through to the highest heaven, let us
> hold firm to our profession of faith. For
> the high priest we have is not incapable
> of feeling our weaknesses with us, but
> has been put to the test in exactly the
> same way as ourselves, apart from sin.
> Let us, then, approach the throne of
> grace with confidence to receive mercy
> and to find grace in time of need.
>
> *Hebrews 4:14-16*

First: if you are going through physical or mental
suffering right now, but you are reading this
book, then you are reaching out and thinking
about something beyond your own personal
pain. This shows courage and grace. God is with
you. Hang on.

No matter how strong our faith, it cannot
insulate us from suffering. The nineteenth-
century Jesuit priest and poet Gerard Manley
Hopkins wrote six sonnets that are often
referred to as the 'terrible sonnets', not because

they lack quality, far from it, but because they so vividly express his feelings of profound anguish. The sonnet, *No worst, there is none. Pitched past pitch of grief* contains lines which have become well known for conveying the frightening reality of mental illness.

> O the mind, mind has mountains; cliffs of fall
> Frightful, sheer, no-man-fathomed. Hold
>   them cheap
> May who ne'er hung there.
>
> *Gerald Manley Hopkins*[1]

Very few of us will get through our lives without experiencing some form of suffering. Because disability and illness are an integral part of being human, so, inevitably, is suffering. Of course, some people will ask, if God loves us and is all-powerful, why does God let us suffer? Thinking about this means thinking about what it is to be a human being, and our place in the world.

In his book *The Problem of Pain*, C. S. Lewis wrote:

> The inexorable 'laws of Nature' which operate in defiance of human suffering or desert, which are not turned aside by prayer, seem at first sight, to furnish a strong argument against the goodness and power of God. I am going to submit that not even Omnipotence could create a society of free souls without at the same time creating a relatively independent and 'inexorable' Nature.[2]

Some people may find the idea of these inexorable laws of nature, indifferent to our personal wellbeing, rather disturbing, but Lewis describes these laws as being like the unvarying rules in a game of chess – without them, the game is impossible. If players could move their chess pieces around the board just as they felt like, there would really be no point in even starting a game.

And of course, much human suffering is caused by other human beings, through conflict, violence, greed, and selfishness. We can never completely eliminate the suffering which is sometimes the inevitable product of people exercising their free will. Whether it is the heartbreak of a relationship breakdown or the devastation that may be caused by a careless driver, we cannot stop it all – if we did, human beings would be little more than automatons. If we exclude suffering from the world, said Lewis, we exclude life itself.

But just as human beings can cause much suffering, they can also do a lot to keep suffering to a minimum. By dedicating adequate resources to medical research, healthcare, social security, and social care support, the impact of those inexorable laws of nature on our health and wellbeing can be kept to a minimum. By demanding that politicians prioritise these issues, and by voting accordingly, we can all play our part in this. By exercising social responsibility instead of prioritising our own interests, we can help to keep suffering to a minimum, and where suffering cannot be avoided, we can ensure that maximum support is given to those who suffer and the people caring for them.

The Old Testament is full of stories of profound suffering and struggle, often on an epic scale. Extremely dramatic and packed with incident, they have been told and retold over the centuries, through art and literature, on stage and screen, becoming embedded in our culture. We don't need to have studied the Bible to be familiar with the story of Noah's Ark, or be able to hum a tune from *Joseph and the Amazing Technicolour Dreamcoat*.

Perhaps the most extended and intense account of suffering in the Old Testament is the Book of Job. Job is a good and righteous man who suffers in every imaginable way. Showing formidable endurance and resilience, he refuses to blame God, but cries out in anguish for an explanation. In return, he is not given a direct or easy answer, but an overwhelming and awe-inspiring experience of the power and majesty of God, described in what is widely acknowledged as one of the world's great poetic masterpieces. The magnificent sweep of this poem puts Job's suffering into a context of immeasurable vastness and grandeur, as described by Frank Cottrell-Boyce in his study guide on forgiveness in this series.[3]

The book of Job is followed by the Psalms, and at the beginning of Psalm 22 we read another anguished cry:

> My God, my God, why have you
> forsaken me?
> Why is your rescue far from me,
> so far from my words of anguish?
> O my God, I call by day and you do not
> answer;
> I call by night and I find no relief.
> *Psalm 22*

You no doubt noticed that the words in the opening line of this psalm are the words later spoken by Jesus on the Cross. As so often happens in the Old Testament, this is a foreshadowing of what is to come, when a God who is majestic and magnificent but remote becomes, through the incarnation, fully human in Jesus. Through Jesus we encounter a God of empathy and com-passion – a God who is literally suffering with us.

In the New Testament, suffering is experienced on a human rather than an epic scale, and recounted in a far more personal way, which we may find easier to relate to than the dramatic tales from the Old Testament. In Jesus, God is no longer distant and immutable, he experiences what human beings experience, and so can understand our joys and sorrows.

The Franciscan writer Richard Rohr says something about suffering which many Christians may find shocking, but which I find both liberating and reassuring. He says,

I have come to believe that Jesus's solidarity with suffering on the cross, is actually *an acceptance of a certain meaninglessness in the universe*, its nonsensical tragic nature, a black hole that seems constantly to show itself to sensitive souls. To accept some degree of meaninglessness is our final and full act of faith that God is still good and still in control.[4]

This feels true to me, and I find it liberating because I think it relieves us of the burden of trying to understand or find a reason for everything. As we discussed in an earlier chapter, illness and disability are not visited on us for any reason, they are not punishments, they simply happen as a manifestation of the infinite variety and diversity of life, so to seek a reason or a meaning for our suffering can be distressing and counterproductive. If we can accept that not everything that happens to us has to have a meaning or a reason, we no longer ask 'why?', or 'why me?', but simply accept what comes along, with the knowledge that whatever it is, a loving God is there with us.

Questions for reflection
- If you have suffered, did you feel there was a reason for it, or a purpose?
- What in your life has caused you the greatest suffering? What helped you to get through it or made it more bearable?
- Did you feel God was with you in your suffering, or did you feel alone?

2 LIVING WITH SUFFERING

> Then Jesus came with them to a plot of
> land called Gethsemane; and he said to
> his disciples, 'Sit here while I go over
> there to pray.' He took Peter and the
> two sons of Zebedee with him. And he
> began to feel sadness and anguish. Then
> he said to them, 'My soul is sorrowful to
> the point of death. Wait here and stay
> awake with me.' And going on a little
> further he fell on his face and prayed,
> saying, 'My Father, if it is possible, let
> this cup pass from me. Only not as I
> want, but as you.
>
> *Matthew 26:36-40*

Ultimately Jesus accepts what is to come, and
places himself in the hands of his Father. And
when his suffering was at its height, when Jesus
hung on the cross in what must have been
intense agony, he finally cried out, 'Father, into
your hands I commit my spirit.' He let go, as we
all must let go in the end.

So, while faith cannot protect us from
suffering, it can, if we allow it, shape how we
feel about it, and how we cope with it. Through
Jesus, God no longer stands above our suffering,
but has entered into it fully and completely.
This solidarity with the pain of the world means
that as Christians we do not have to feel that we
suffer alone – God is with us.

When we are suffering, often what exacerbates it is the feeling, or the fear, that we are not in control. To some extent, we have to accept that we are not. We should of course seek the best possible treatment, pain relief and support that is available, but there will probably be some symptoms of illness or disease which we cannot control or escape. If we willingly hand ourselves over to God, as Jesus did, we may find that the situation is less overwhelming. This of course is far easier said than done.

When we are in the midst of physical pain or mental anguish, we need help, and we need the kind of help that does not demand too much of us. If we reach out to God in prayer, no matter how incoherent or feeble, we may find the help we need:

> Nevertheless, the Spirit too helps us in our weakness, for while we do not know how to pray as we ought, the Spirit personally joins in with unspoken groans; and he who searches hearts knows the mind of the Spirit because the Spirit is joining in on behalf of the saints in accordance with God's will.
>
> *Romans 8:26-27*

In difficult times, I have found one type of prayer most helpful. When I was a child, I was occasionally taken to church when the rosary was being recited. There weren't many people taking part and the church, in my memory, was dark, cold and draughty. It was not an experience I enjoyed, and I found the repetitive nature of the prayer very unengaging. The recitation seemed mechanical and, to my shame, I felt that it was just people going through the motions without much thought.

Now that I am older, I think very differently about that kind of prayer. During spells in hospital, when it was almost impossible to sleep and I was anxious and afraid, the rhythm of the rosary and other familiar prayers could help to calm my mind and give me a feeling of security. It got me through many nights which otherwise would have been quite bleak. Similarly, I found short prayers that could be repeated in my mind like a mantra helpful when I was being wheeled into an operating theatre, or nervously anticipating a painful procedure. This way of reaching out and connecting to God, in a way that is undemanding and comfortingly familiar, is very different from more contemplative prayer, but I now understand that it is in no way less valuable or authentic.

This became even more apparent to me some years ago when, after surgery, I became quite ill. For a while I was in intensive care and unconscious, but as I regained consciousness the first awareness that came to me, before opening my eyes, was that in my head I was halfway through the Lord's Prayer. In what could have been a very confusing and frightening situation, as I took in the strange surroundings, this gave me reassurance, and I really felt that God was with me.

Similarly, there will be times when we cannot bring ourselves to pray, but the knowledge that other people are praying for us makes a difference. Again, in hospital several years ago, I was due to have a procedure which I was really dreading as I expected it to be quite painful. On the morning of the procedure I awoke anxious and afraid.

As time passed however, rather than becoming increasingly anxious, I got calmer, and felt that this calmness was coming from somewhere else. I was aware that other people would be praying for me, and particularly aware that a Quaker friend would be 'holding me in the Light'. The peace and tranquillity which descended upon me felt like a gift, and I was sure God was with me. As it transpired, the actual procedure was as painful as I'd expected, perhaps even more so, but the whole experience was much less unpleasant than it could have been because of the peace of mind which surrounded it.

Mindful of those inexorable laws of nature, I personally never pray with the expectation that the course of a disease will be changed, other than by medical intervention, or that a broken limb will suddenly heal – but I do believe that we can find courage, and grace, and peace of mind which can help us get through whatever we have to deal with. At times there may be only one way we can cope with our physical and mental suffering: to place ourselves in God's hands, and to endure, knowing he loves us.

When the apostles were persecuted, they often wrote about their suffering in a surprisingly calm and accepting way, as they found courage and consolation in their relationship with Jesus.

> We are subjected to every kind of hardship, but not hindered; we see no way out but we are not at a loss; we are pursued but not abandoned, knocked down, but not destroyed, at every moment we carry with us in our body the death of Jesus so that the life of Jesus, too, may be made visible in our body.'
>
> *2 Corinthians 4:8-10*

Ultimately, in the midst of suffering, there was one truth the apostles clung to, and which we can cling to, and which the Bible reassures us of again and again: nothing can separate us from God's love.

> For I am convinced that neither death nor life, nor angels, nor rulers, nothing already in existence and nothing still to come, nor any power, nor height nor depths, nor any other created thing will be able to separate us from the love of God in Christ Jesus our Lord.
>
> *Romans 8:38-39*

We began this chapter by looking at one of Gerard Manley Hopkins' 'terrible sonnets', expressions of desperate anguish. A few years later, not long before he died, Hopkins was able to write a very different poem, with closing lines that are quite extraordinary:

> I am all at once what Christ is,
> since he was what I am, and
> This Jack, joke, poor potsherd,
> patch, matchwood, immortal diamond,
> Is immortal diamond.[5]

As a society we can do much to prevent avoidable suffering, through good social security, healthcare and social care. But ultimately, for most people, there will be suffering we must simply endure. If we can find the strength or the grace to place ourselves in God's hands, we may find it easier to bear. But even if we can't, God will still be with us.

Questions for reflection
- When you are suffering, do you find it difficult to pray?
- How do you pray, what are your expectations, and does it help?
- Does it help if you know people are praying for you?

TAKING IT FURTHER
The Disability and Jesus website hosts An Ordinary Office, which is used daily by many

people who, for all kinds of reasons, are unable to go to church. When online participants finish a prayer they click on Amen, becoming part of an online community in which people pray 'alone, together'. There is also the option to get a member of the team to pray for or with them. It is all completely anonymous, as the team says: 'God is listening. And He knows who you are. We don't need to.'

As a group commit to taking part in the Ordinary Office for a week, focus your prayer on the needs of all those who are suffering and in pain through illness and disability. If this includes some members of the group, please ask if they would like prayers too. You can find the Ordinary Office here: http://anordinaryoffice.org.uk/

At your next session discuss what the experience was like and whether it has helped further your understanding of other people's suffering or isolation.

CULTURE
'Musée des Beaux Arts' is a poem by W. H. Auden, a reflection on the painting *The Fall of Icarus* by Peter Brueghel. Both the painting and poem reflect on how suffering often happens out of view, while ordinary life continues. It is worth studying them together and thinking about what poet and artist are saying about suffering.

A Burnt-out Case, The Heart of the Matter, The Power and the Glory by Graham Greene. Graham Greene was a novelist and 'Catholic agnostic' whose work often focussed on suffering, sin and redemption. In these three different novels, his protagonists struggle with depression, ill health, faith, and relationships. While Greene never has easy answers, his books get to the heart of the human condition.

Ethan Frome by Edith Wharton tells the story of a man trapped in a marriage to woman who is ill. He falls in love with her cousin but when they plan a suicide pact, worse suffering is to follow.

The Problem of Pain by C. S. Lewis. In this work of non-fiction Lewis wrestles with what it means to suffer.

PRAYER

God of Compassion,
You suffered on the cross and you know our pain.
Help us to endure the suffering we cannot avoid,
And comfort us with the knowledge of your loving presence.

NOTES

1. Gerard Manley Hopkins, 'No worst, there is none, pitched past pitch of grief', taken from *Gerard Manley Hopkins: Poems and Prose* (1985) and reproduced on the Poetry Foundation website: https://www.poetryfoundation.org/poems/44398/no-worst-there-is-none-pitched-past-pitch-of-grief

2. C. S. Lewis, *The Problem of Pain* (The Centenary Press, 1940)

3. Frank Cottrell-Boyce, *How the Bible Can Help Us Understand Forgiveness* (Darton Longman and Todd, 2020)

4. Richard Rohr, *Eager to Love: The Alternative Way of Francis of Assisi* (Hodder & Stoughton, 2014)

5. Gerald Manley Hopkins, 'That Nature is a Heraclitean Fire and of the comfort of the Resurrection', taken from *Gerald Manley Hopkins: Poems and Prose* (1985) and reproduced on the Poetry Foundation website: https://www.poetryfoundation.org/poems/44397/that-nature-is-a-heraclitean-fire-and-of-the-comfort-of-the-resurrection

5

THE GIFT AND THE CHALLENGE OF CARING

1 LOVE THY NEIGHBOUR

But he was anxious to justify himself and said to Jesus, 'And who is my neighbour?' In answer Jesus said, 'A man was on his way down from Jerusalem to Jericho and fell into the hands of bandits; they stripped him, beat him and then made off, leaving him half dead. Now by chance a priest was travelling down the same road, but when he saw the man, he passed by on the other side. In the same way a Levite who came to the place saw him, and passed by on the other side. But a Samaritan traveller who came on him was moved with compassion when he saw him. He went up to him and bandaged his wounds, pouring oil and wine on them. He then lifted him onto his own mount and took him to an inn and looked after him. Next day, he took out two denarii and handed them to the innkeeper and said, 'Look after him, and on my way back I will make good any extra expense.' Which of these three, do you think, proved himself a neighbour to the man who fell into the bandits' hands?' He replied, 'The one who showed mercy towards him.' Jesus said to him, 'Go, and do the same yourself.'

Luke 10:29-37

Loving each other and caring for one another is such a fundamental principle of Christianity, and such an undisputed one, that it does not seem necessary to examine it here. As Christians, and as human beings, caring for each other is the foundation on which our lives are built. As the old Irish proverb says, 'It is in the shelter of each other that the people live.' But being 'a carer', helping another person facing physical or mental challenges to live their life on a daily basis, is a special and distinct role, which can be the dominant role in a person's life for years, even decades. It is that role which we will be exploring here.

Just as few of us will avoid being ill or disabled at some time in our lives, so most of us will also take on, to a greater or lesser extent, the role of a carer. It may be the most demanding role many of us will ever undertake. It can be physically, mentally, and emotionally exhausting, as numerous practical tasks may be combined with the anguish of seeing a loved one go through physical or mental suffering which we cannot stop. Being a carer can also bring poverty and hardship. Cumulatively, it can have an enormous impact, and change how we think and feel about many things.

If asked to name a Bible story about caring for others, I imagine many people would say the Good Samaritan. Not walking by on the other side of the road, and being a good Samaritan are expressions which have become part of our language, used by many people who may not even be familiar with the Bible story. Let's look at what actually happens.

What struck me about reading the story afresh was that the Samaritan gave emergency assistance to the man and got him to a place of safety, but beyond the first twenty-four hours, he didn't actually physically do the caring work himself. What he did do, with kindness and generosity, was take responsibility for the man's care. It seems to me that the story is about physically caring for a person in the first instance, but then it is about taking responsibility, in a way which involves a financial commitment and sharing of resources. It is physical caring and social responsibility, with both equally important.

Jesus tells us through this parable that really anyone in need is our neighbour. We don't have to know them, live near them, or be related to them to have responsibility for them. While we may be more closely involved in caring for members of our own family, we also have a responsibility to the wider community. In our modern society, we can help fulfil this responsibility by ensuring that our NHS and social care system is properly funded, with good quality care available to all who need it.

The Good Samaritan is immediately followed by the story of Martha and Mary, which I think also says much about different ways of caring, the physical and emotional labour involved, and the dilemmas carers can face.

> In the course of their journey he came to a village, and a woman named Martha welcomed him into her house. She had a sister called Mary, who sat down at the Lord's feet and listened to him speaking. Now Martha, who was distracted with all the serving, came to him and said, 'Lord, do you not care that my sister is leaving me to do the serving all by myself? Then tell her to help me. But the Lord answered, 'Martha, Martha,' he said, 'you worry and fret about so many things, and yet few are needed, indeed only one. It is Mary who has chosen the better part, and it is not to be taken from her.'
>
> *Luke 10:38-42*

To be honest, for many years I had a problem with this particular Bible story. Like the story of the prodigal son, where the good son seems to be taken for granted and the repentant prodigal is celebrated, it felt a bit unfair. Intellectually I understood the point that was being made, but I still felt annoyed on Martha's behalf. Left to do all the domestic work while Mary appears to be taking it easy, it is only natural that Martha should feel rather aggrieved. Then, when she understandably complains, Jesus tells her that it is actually Mary who is playing the more important role. I heartily sympathised with Martha.

My understanding changed considerably, however, after being involved, to a very limited extent, in caring for my Mum before she died. I tried to do what I could, but my own limitations meant I had to leave much to my brothers. After my Mum died, I came to realise that it would probably have been better if I had tried to do even less in a practical way – been less like Martha, and more like Mary. Just spending time with Mum, listening and talking, being fully present for her, would probably have been more beneficial. So, the story of Martha and Mary suddenly made sense to me. As the philosopher Simone Weil said, attention is the rarest and purest form of generosity. When caring for people who are ill, sometimes it is impossible to avoid our caring becoming a hard and tiring job, which leaves little time for simply paying attention to that person as an individual, as we naturally do with others for whom we care, but are not actually 'caring'.

It can be impossible to give people this quality of attention they need and deserve without sufficient practical assistance. In the latter years of Mum's life, we were able to support her as a family on a day to day basis without outside help. As her life drew to a close though, we were extremely privileged to have the assistance of some wonderfully compassionate district nurses and healthcare assistants who provided palliative care. These exceptional people came into Mum's home several times a day and provided all the personal and medical care that she needed, allowing us to just be her family again. This was a great gift, and they truly did seem like angels, as the weight lifted off our shoulders and we were able, at the end, to just sit and hold Mum's hand and hope that she could feel the enormous love we had for her. This was caring given and received as a gift, for which we will be eternally grateful.

This experience with my Mum made me appreciate how nurses, professional care workers, and family members can all make unique and different contributions to the care of a person who needs a lot of support. For example, some people may be embarrassed to have a family member involved in very intimate care, and having a professional person do those tasks feels more dignified – others may feel the exact opposite. Round the clock care may be impossible to sustain for family members, particularly if they themselves are older or not in good health. In some circumstances, safety requirements may dictate that a residential care home is the only option. The ideal situation is to have a full range of professional and family care available which can then be tailored to an individual's requirements. When the balance is right, dignity is preserved and wellbeing is nurtured. But when the balance is wrong, as we shall see in the next section, then the consequences can be severe.

Questions for reflection

- In the story of Martha and Mary, with whom do you identify more closely?
- How do you think other people see you – as a Martha or a Mary?
- Does it matter if you are one or the other? Can you be both?

2   THE STRUGGLE TO CARE

> Children, be obedient to your parents in the Lord – that is right. Honour your father and your mother is the first commandment with a promise so that you may prosper and have long life on earth. And parents, do not provoke children to anger but nourish them with discipline and the instruction of the Lord.
>
> *Ephesians 6:1-4*

Unfortunately, for some people the experience of being a carer can be very difficult – indeed to call it a challenge is something of an understatement.

In recent years, a rising demand for adult social care has been accompanied by big cuts to funding, so fewer family carers receive the support they need. In October 2019, commenting on the latest official figures, Helen Walker, Chief Executive at Carers UK said:

Appallingly, this is the fifth consecutive year we've seen fewer carers in England supported by their local authority, with 22 per cent fewer supported or assessed this year compared to five years ago.

Despite breaks being essential for carers' wellbeing, the number receiving respite has also reduced by almost a quarter.

The fast-diminishing support for unpaid carers is simply not good enough at a time when more and more family members are having to step in to care for loved ones. Unpaid carers are propping up our crumbling social care system and being left without vital practical support and much-needed breaks from caring.[1]

This lack of support from society places enormous pressure on carers, often to the detriment of their own health. Recent research found that a third of carers, given some precious time off, would use it to see a doctor about their own health, which they have been neglecting, or to catch up on some much-needed sleep.[2]

Financial pressures can also be very damaging to the wellbeing of carers. In 2019 a

report from Carers UK said that over the past
two years, 600 people a day had given up their
job to take up caring responsibilities.[3] At the
time of writing, UK Carers Allowance is a mere
£66.15 per week, and only payable if people
spend at least 35 hours per week on their caring
duties. Too often, as with disability, caring and
poverty are inextricably linked.

Professional care workers are also poorly
paid and often employed on unfair terms and
conditions. In 2019 it was reported that many
who visit people in their homes are paid below
the minimum wage, because they are not paid
for their travel time between clients.[4]

This financial reality indicates the value
which society currently places on the caring role.
Just as we should not hold up disabled people as
inspiring examples whilst denying their rights,
we shouldn't laud the virtues but neglect the
needs of those who take on a caring role. When
this happens, as we shall see from Kate's story,
the damage can be profound.

Kate, married with four children of school
age, was a carer for both her parents for eight
years before they died. She told me she found
the experience 'grim, traumatic, and at times
almost unbearable'. Several years after she
stopped being a carer she is still trying to recover,
both emotionally and financially.

As her parents entered a physical and
mental decline, their attitude towards Kate
became less loving and increasingly hostile
and abusive. They lived nearby and she visited

them several times a day, often being greeted by, 'You're looking fat' or 'You look a state', which gradually eroded her self-esteem and her confidence. They were suspicious of strangers and would not countenance paid carers coming into their home, so as the demands on her time increased Kate felt she had no alternative but to give up her job, at a crucial point in her career. She rapidly felt 'dragged down' to living the life of an octogenarian, as days revolved around medication, medical appointments, and a diet of her parents' favourite television programmes about frauds, cheats and rip-offs, which only made them more distrustful.

Without Kate's salary, her own household fell into mounting debt, but she could not claim Carers' Allowance because her parents refused to acknowledge that they were dependent, or that she was their carer – she was just their daughter, doing what a daughter was expected to do. Money became a constant worry, and Kate vividly recalls the time she did her parents' shopping, showed them the receipts, and said, 'You owe me £70', to which her mother replied aggressively, 'I owe you nothing!'

All the time, Kate was telling herself that her parents had had a difficult life and were now frail, vulnerable, and afraid – but still their attitude towards her, and their cruel words, made her feel unhappy and worthless. She also felt enormous guilt, because due to the mounting pressures she often found herself wondering how long this would continue –

speculating about when her parents might die, knowing that the longer they lived, the worse everything would get. Kate's husband was very supportive, but she was keenly aware of the impact on him and the children. She recalls her daughter saying, 'You may have had a horrible time with Gran, but don't take it out on me.'

Although Kate still loved her parents, and knew in theory that she was doing the best she could in the circumstances, she constantly reproached herself for her feelings of resentment. She was doing what she thought was the right thing, and what everybody else thought was the right thing, but often found herself wondering, 'Why don't I feel like a good person?'

Asked if anything positive came out of her experience as a carer, Kate says it made her appreciate even more the kindness of her husband, and his unmaterialistic nature. They are still struggling with the financial problems which built up when Kate couldn't work, but he never complains about it. And after spending so much time in hospitals and GP surgeries, she says she is now quite an expert at navigating the NHS and being assertive when necessary.

Spiritually, Kate says that in some of her darkest times, when she wished that her parents could be loving parents, the knowledge that Jesus did love her unconditionally was something she clung to. She now gets great solace from attending church and feels that God is healing the hurt and damage she incurred during that time. She is recovering her peace of mind but has been left with a profound sense of anger.

Kate is angry at the way society pays lip service to unpaid carers, whilst openly celebrating the amount of money they save the public purse. She is even more angry when the churches go along with this and do not speak up for them. She believes that by sanctifying the caring role, and praising carers without demanding more support and more resources for them, the church is 'colluding with the exploitation of vulnerable people'. It is a political, economic and structural problem, which will not be solved without political pressure.

And of course, family carers love the people they are caring for, so they rarely complain because they don't want their loved ones to feel they are a burden. For someone to admit they find caring too hard feels like breaking a taboo. But, says Kate, the church could break that taboo on their behalf, and let people know that if they need to walk away, just for a while or even permanently, then that does not make them a bad or selfish person.

Kate often thinks of the passage from Ephesians quoted at the top of this section. The first part is familiar to most people, even those who aren't particularly religious. It has passed into our culture and can contribute to the pressure felt by people whose parents need care. But Kate thinks the third sentence, less often quoted, is also important and should be remembered by carers who are struggling. The relationship between adult children and dependent parents can be extremely difficult, and if those children feel angry or resentful, it is often a perfectly natural reaction to the situation they are in, not something to be judged or condemned.

At the moment, Kate feels that carers are being 'sacrificed on the altar of Mammon'. When politicians and clergy praise them but do little to help them, she thinks of the scribes and Pharisees in this passage from Matthew,

> 'Then addressing the crowds and his disciples Jesus said, 'The scribes and the Pharisees occupy the chair of Moses. You must therefore do and observe everything that they tell you; but do not do what they do, since they do not practise what they teach. They tie up heavy burdens and lay them on people's shoulders, but they do not lift a finger to move them.'
>
> *Matthew 23:4*

Kate is particularly concerned about the plight of young carers, children who are looking after an ill or disabled parent. They often pay a high price emotionally, socially, and in terms of their education and life chances. Referring to Luke 14:26, where Jesus says:

> 'Anyone who comes to me without hating father, mother, wife, children, brothers, sisters, yes and even life itself, cannot be my disciple'
>
> *Luke 14:26*

Kate says,

> The Bible says we must honour our father and mother, but it also makes clear that following Jesus must outweigh all other considerations. Maybe for some people, the experience of being a carer can get in the way of knowing that they are precious and loved by Jesus. Maybe, for a carer, putting Jesus first may mean admitting when the caring role is too much for them – and perhaps, for the church, following Jesus involves ensuring, as far as we can, that nobody's burden is too heavy for them to bear.

Having reflected on her experience, and prayed about it, Kate concludes,

> I wasn't brave enough to ignore my parents, and maybe that was right, and God gave me the strength to see it through to the end, and I can't think what else I could have done – but I would still like other people to have permission to stop and say it is hurting too much. Especially younger people without

the supportive partner and children and positive life experiences I had – to be able to ignore the bad advice and not feel they were put into the world to rescue people.

Just as we need to build a society in which ill and disabled people can thrive, so we also need to ensure that carers are not crushed by the responsibility of caring, but are supported so that they can give those who need it their full and loving attention, while maintaining their own health and wellbeing. This requires government to provide support through the social security system to ensure that caring does not lead to debt and financial hardship. Government also needs to ensure that where it is not practical for people to be cared for by a family member, good quality social care is available either in their own home or in a residential care home setting, whichever is appropriate. And family carers need support and the opportunity to have a break, so that caring does not become an oppressive burden.

The stories of the Good Samaritan and of Martha and Mary show how the task of the carer can be shared and eased, if we all take responsibility together. When society doesn't take responsibility and fails to support carers, the caring role can become impossibly difficult and demanding. This can eventually lead to resentment of those who need care.

Caring should be a social as well as a personal responsibility, and we can exercise this collective social responsibility through local and national government policies and spending.

The coronavirus pandemic brought with it a deeper appreciation of the invaluable work of everyone involved in our NHS and social care. Workers who had for years been low paid and treated with little consideration or respect suddenly became 'key workers', their jobs recognised as essential. It is to be hoped that this new appreciation continues when the pandemic is over, and society will supply the resources necessary to make paid and unpaid carers' lives less difficult

A combination of the compassionate social responsibility shown by the Good Samaritan, and the practical care provided by Martha can, ideally, leave loved ones free to give the attention that Mary paid to Jesus in the parable, and which he stressed was so important.

> 'By this everyone will know that
> you are my disciples
> if you have love for one another.'
> *John 13:35*

Questions for reflection
- Have you had experience of being a carer/being cared for or know someone who has? What is that experience like?
- Who should be responsible for caring for our family members who are sick or disabled?

- What do you think stops people from caring for relatives? What helps them?

TAKING IT FURTHER

Most areas have a local voluntary organisation which endeavours to help and support carers. See if you can find one in your area and ask if they can provide a speaker to talk about their work, or if there is a way you can get involved in any of their fundraising or social activities.

CULTURE

The Life of Florence Nightingale: The Courageous life of a legendary nurse by Catherine Reef. Clarion Bools. Florence Nightingale is an iconic carer, but the popular image of her has been rather sanitised. Not only did she care for injured troops, she was very active politically in order to bring about better conditions which would lessen their suffering and prevent disease. In the latter part of her life she became bedbound and so was cared for herself, but she continued lobbying and campaigning from her bed and remained very influential.

We're Sorry We Missed You is a film written by Paul Greengrass and directed by Ken Loach, which shows the struggles of a family in which the mother is a professional care worker.

'Felix Randall' is a poem by the Jesuit priest Gerard Manley Hopkins, an intensely moving account of the relationship between a sick

person and the priest who offers comfort in his final days, and the love and mutual dependency in that relationship.

Human Chain is a book of poems written by Seamus Heaney after he had suffered a stroke. One poem, *Miracle*, is based on the story of the paralysed man healed by Jesus, and focuses on the hard, physical effort of the friends who lowered the man through the roof into Jesus's presence.

Dog Ears by Anne Booth, is a book about a young carer who confides in her dog.

PRAYER

> God of Mercy,
> You told us that when we care for others, we
>   are caring for you.
> Help us to be patient and kind,
> To ask for help when we need it,
> And to forgive ourselves when we feel we are
>   failing,
> As you will always forgive us.

NOTES

1. Carers UK Press release, *Fifth fewer unpaid carers being supported by local authorities in England*, 22 October 2019. Carer's UK website: https://www.carersuk.org/news-and-campaigns/press-releases/fifth-fewer-unpaid-carers-being-supported-by-local-authorities-in-england

2. Carers UK September 2019: https://www.carersuk.org/news-and-campaigns/press-releases/third-of-unpaid-carers-would-use-a-break-from-caring-to-see-the-doctor

3. Carer's UK Report, *Juggling work and unpaid care: A growing issue*: https://www.carersuk.org/news-and-campaigns/press-releases/more-than-600-people-quit-work-to-look-after-older-and-disabled-relatives-every-day

4. Angeline Albert, *Majority of home care workers paid less than the minimum wage* Homecare.co.uk, 30 January 2019: https://www.homecare.co.uk/news/article.cfm/id/1605174/Most-home-care-workers-are-paid-less-than-minimum-wage

6

REFRAINING FROM JUDGEMENT: LOGS AND SPLINTERS

1 HEALTH AND LIFESTYLE

He spoke the following parable to some people who prided themselves on being righteous, and despised everyone else, 'Two men went up to the Temple to pray, one a Pharisee, the other a tax collector. The Pharisee stood there and said this prayer to himself, "I thank you, God, that I am not grasping, unjust, adulterous like everyone else, and particularly that I am not like this tax collector here. I fast twice a week; I pay tithes on all I possess." The tax collector stood at a distance, not daring even to raise his eyes to heaven; but he beat his breast and said, "God, be merciful to me, a sinner." This man, I tell you, went

home again justified; the other did not.
For everyone who raises himself up will
be humbled, but anyone who humbles
himself will be raised up.'

Luke 18:9-14

There is a growing tendency to view some
illnesses as being, to a greater or lesser extent,
due to poor lifestyle choices which represent
a form of moral failing. For example, obesity
and the diseases which accompany it are often
portrayed as the result of stupidity, laziness, or
gluttony.[1] People with an addiction problem are
condemned as lacking self-discipline, and those
whose addiction involves illegal substances are
criminalised and stigmatised.[2]

People who pride themselves on living a
healthy lifestyle may feel morally superior to
those who don't. But throughout the gospels we
see that Jesus is not impressed by people who
consider themselves superior in this way.

Whenever ill health is spoken of as being
the result of poor personal choices, justice and
humility oblige us to consider what are known
as the social determinants of health. These are
the conditions in which people are born, grow,
work, live, and age – the wider forces which
shape their lives. Social determinants make
it relatively easy for some people to have a
long and healthy life, while making it almost
impossible for others. When we take these

factors into consideration, it becomes clear that a judgemental attitude towards ill health is not only lacking in compassion, it is often quite unfounded and unjust.

There is a clear and well documented link between poverty, disadvantage, and ill health, manifested most starkly in the difference in life expectancy between the rich and the poor. The most recent figures from the Office for National Statistics tell us that in England, the difference in life expectancy between the least and most deprived people was 9 years for males and 7 years for females.[3] These however are average figures for the whole country. When we take a closer look at the most and least deprived areas in individual regions or cities, the differences are more dramatic. In London for instance, the difference in life expectancy between rich and poor areas can be 25 years.[4]

Perhaps what is even more relevant to our considerations are the figures on Healthy Life Expectancy, or Disability Free Life Expectancy. As the Office for National Statistics baldly states: 'Healthy life expectancy at birth among males living in the most deprived areas in England was 51.7 years, compared with 70.4 years among the least deprived, almost two fewer decades of life in "Good" general health.'[5]

So, we see, when it comes to health and lifestyle, the gospel advice not to stand in judgement over others is very pertinent.

One of the most important factors which contributes to health inequality is the ability to access a healthy diet. Public Health England has published *The Eatwell Guide*, official government guidance on a diet that meets all our nutritional needs. For a household to be able to eat this way, they must be able to afford the foods recommended, and have the resources and facilities to cook them.

In September 2018, the Food Foundation researched the affordability of this diet, and concluded that for households in the bottom ten per cent of the income scale, almost three-quarters of their disposable income would need to be spent on food in order to eat in the recommended way. In low income households with children, the amount they would need to spend to eat this healthy diet would leave very little money left to pay for electricity, gas, shoes, clothes, transport, toiletries etc. In contrast, those at the top of the income scale would need to spend only 6 per cent of their income to eat healthily.[6]

And of course, to buy that good nutritional food, one has to get to a shop that sells it. Some deprived areas have been dubbed 'food deserts', as fresh food is not available without access to a car or bus – and bus fares reduce the amount of money available to spend on food when you get to the shop, thus compounding the problem. So we can see that if we judge people for having an unhealthy diet, we may be looking at only part of the picture, and humility may require us to look a little deeper.

'I have come so that they may have life
and have it in plenty.'

John 10:10

We know that God loves each and every one
of us and wants us all to live our life in the
best way possible. As we are members of one
body, we have a responsibility to help each
other to live a good and healthy life. So, we
need to try to ensure that society is organised
in such way as to make this possible. Early
Christian communities gave us a model for the
type of society in which everyone can thrive,
through a radical form of charity and selfless
giving which could be summed up as, 'From
each according to his ability, to each according
to his needs'.

And all the believers were united and
owned everything in common; they sold
their goods and possessions and divided
the proceeds to all according to what
each one needed. Each day, with one
heart, they went faithfully to the Temple
but met in their houses for the breaking
of bread; they ate their share of food
with glad and generous hearts, praising
God and approved by all the people.

Acts 2:44-46

In a small community we can see that this radical and informal sharing worked well, and everyone was happy. But in a large modern society, we clearly need more formal arrangements to make sure everyone is provided for. Charity is not the answer, for several reasons. It does not enhance anyone's dignity to be reliant on charity, as people who find themselves at a foodbank will testify. Also, not surprisingly, charitable wealth and resources are disproportionately concentrated in affluent areas, leaving the most deprived communities struggling, as people who might themselves be in poverty try to help those who are destitute.[7] If wealth and resources are going to be shared in a fair way then it needs to be done on a national scale and in a more formal manner, probably through a system of taxation and redistribution. Like the early Christian community, but on a much larger scale.

Questions for reflection
- Do you know people who are struggling to afford a good diet? If you yourself are struggling to afford healthy food, do you feel able to talk about it with the group?
- Do you think this inequality of life span is talked about enough?
- What responsibility do we have for this inequality in health and life span?

2 THE PROBLEM OF ADDICTION

> Brothers and sisters, even if someone is caught in some fault, those of you who are spiritual should set that person right in a spirit of gentleness; and watch yourself that you are not tempted too. Carry one another's burdens, and in this way you will fulfil the law of Christ. Someone who thinks himself important, when he is not, deceives himself; but each one should examine his own work and so have cause for boasting for himself and not for anyone else. Each one has a personal load to carry.
>
> *Galatians 6:1-5*

Addiction is another health issue where people are often judgemental. However, there is a growing understanding of the link between addiction problems and traumatic experiences. The Chief Executive of the military mental health charity Combat Stress, Sue Reeth, says, 'As many as 43 per cent of veterans registered with Combat Stress have a current problem with alcohol misuse. From the conversations we have had with veterans being supported by Combat Stress, we're all too aware that many of the veterans use alcohol or drugs to help them to manage their trauma and emotional health.' This is really not a 'lifestyle choice'.[8]

One in Four UK is a charity that specialises

in supporting survivors of sexual abuse and trauma, particularly childhood abuse. In 2019 they published a report, *Numbing the Pain: Survivors' voices of childhood sexual abuse and addiction* [9] in which fourteen men and women, aged from their 20s to their 60s, explained how they turned to alcohol and drugs to help them cope with what had happened to them as children. Their stories are disturbing and very moving. Thomas says,

> I am not a bad man. I am a man who has suffered horrific childhood sexual abuse, neglect and abandonment at the hands of the people who should have been keeping me safe and showing me love.

He started to self-medicate with alcohol, then moved to drugs, which made him happy for the first time in his life.

> The drugs took all my pain away and produced blissful euphoria. I was enslaved. I couldn't get enough, and I couldn't stop.

In the foreword to the report, Chip Somers, a psychotherapist who has worked with people with addiction and dependency problems for more than 30 years, says he believes that a large proportion of his clients were sexually abused as children.

> I do not believe it to be the cause of addiction, but it is a significant factor amongst many,

that combine to make someone so ill at ease with themselves that the anaesthetic benefit of drugs and alcohol is like a siren call.[10]

Of course, it is very important to note that not all people with an addiction problem have experienced abuse or trauma, and not everyone who has experienced abuse or trauma will develop an addiction problem. But when we see a person in the grip of drug or alcohol dependency, it may be all too easy to criticise them for a lack of will power or self-discipline. We may actually be standing in judgement over someone who is trying to numb an intense emotional, psychological and spiritual pain.

As Paul says, we all have a personal load to carry. We can help one another to carry our burdens, and where appropriate set people right in a spirit of gentleness. But we are not entitled to judge with a sense of superiority.

And there is growing evidence that the gentle approach towards people with addiction problems, rather than a punitive one, may be the best way. In the 1990s, Portugal had a very serious illegal drugs problem, and the criminal justice approach was not working. In 2001, possession of drugs for personal use was decriminalised. Drug dealing remained a crime, and drug dealers still get sent to prison, but users are now treated very differently. When a person is found in possession of drugs they may be referred to a Commission for the

Dissuasion of Drug Addiction, in the hope that they will be prevented from ever becoming an addict. Their problem is treated as a medical and social problem, rather than a criminal one, and extra resources have been put into more supportive health and welfare policies. Since this change of approach, drug-related deaths and HIV infections have fallen dramatically.[11] Meanwhile, in the UK, the most recent figures for drug-related deaths are the highest on record, and we have a drug death rate twelve times that of Portugal.[12]

> 'Do not judge, and you will not be judged; because the judgements you give are the judgements you will get, and the standard you use will be the standard used for you. Why do you observe the splinter in your brother's eye and never notice the log in your own? And will you say to your brother, 'Let me take that splinter out of your eye,' when, see, there is a log in your own? Hypocrite! Take the log out of your own eye first, and then you will see clearly to take the splinter out of your brother's eye.'
>
> *Matthew 7:1-5*

So, we see that none of us are in a position to stand in judgement over other people and what we may see as their 'poor lifestyle choices'. We do not have the moral right to do so, as Jesus says when he uses the metaphor of the log and the splinter. The gap in healthy life expectancy between rich and poor shows us that personal choice often has very little to do with it – what really counts is social and economic status. We now know that in the areas where poor people can afford to live, even the air tends to be of poorer quality, and so contributes to poorer health.[13]

The relationship between inequality and health was thrown into stark relief by the coronavirus pandemic. While many people on higher incomes were more able to stockpile food and work from home relatively comfortably, those with low incomes, no savings and insecure work were left worrying about how they would cope financially. Even as NHS staff pleaded with people to stay at home, many felt they had no alternative but to take some risks with their health just to survive from week to week, and this undoubtedly helped to spread the virus. It was a painful and tragic reminder that we are indeed all interdependent, and that we really are all members of one body.

In earlier parts of this book we thought about how illness and disability can happen to anyone, and how most of us will be affected at some stage in our lives. The fact that so much illness and disability can be attributed to social and economic inequality is disturbing, but it also means that things can change for the better. If we strive to follow the gospel teachings which we have explored here, by making society more just and more inclusive, we can reduce the suffering experienced by so many people, and build a society in which all can thrive, and live the life God would want them to live.

As it is, the members are many but the body is one. The eye cannot say to the hand, 'I do not need you,' nor can the head say to the feet, 'I do not need you.' What is more, the members of the body that seem to be weaker are indispensable. And the ones we consider less dignified we surround with greater dignity; and the less respectable members are given greater respect which our respectable members do not need. In composing the body God has given honour to the members which were without it, and so that there may not be disagreements inside the body, but all the members should take the same care for one another. If one member is suffering, all the members share its suffering. And if one member is honoured, all the members share its joy.

1 Corinthians 12:20-26

Questions for reflection

- What changes are needed in society to help improve life expectancy for poorer people?
- How can people living with addictions be helped to live a healthier life?
- Do you think inequality can affect the health of the whole community, not just in a pandemic situation, and if so how?

TAKING IT FURTHER

Go to a shop or supermarket within walking distance of your home, with £5 in your pocket, and do some food shopping. Imagine you have little or no gas or electricity available with which to cook, and you need to shop for at least a few days. What choices are available to you, and how do the choices you make differ from your usual choices? Think about the effect of eating like this in the long term.

Find out what would be included in a typical parcel from your local foodbank. Does it constitute a healthy diet?

CULTURE

Royal College of General Practitioners Annual Conference, Lecture by Professor Sir Michael Marmot, October 2019. With warmth and humour the Professor outlines the challenges of health inequality we face in the UK today: https://www.youtube.com/watch?v=0TOV5Ietsdw

BBC Ideas series, a three-minute video with Dr Gabor Mate who talks about addiction as a response to emotional pain. He says the question we should ask an addict is not, 'What is wrong with you?' but 'What happened to you?'
https://www.bbc.com/ideas/videos/addiction-is-a-response-to-emotional-pain/p07tnh6m

The Spirit Level: Why More Equal Societies Almost Always Do Better by Kate Pickett and Richard Wilkinson. The book highlights the pernicious effects that inequality has on a large range of health and social problems.

Stuart: A Life Lived Backwards by Alexander Masters details the friendship between the author and Stuart, a homeless alcoholic, whose suffered difficulties in childhood, and who died aged 33 when he was struck by a train.

The Wire. US TV Series, screenplay by David Simon. *The Wire* is a TV series set in Baltimore that follows the fortunes of police officers, drug dealers, homeless people, dock workers, drug addicts, teachers, pupils, politicians and journalists, trying to make sense of the drug war. Through the eyes of its characters, we see how poverty and deprivation keep those on the wrong side of town from the healthy, happy existence of those with plenty.

PRAYER

God of Wisdom,

Help us to understand lives which may be
very different from our own,

Give us the sensitivity to see pain which
may be hidden,

And help us to refrain from judgement.

May we always challenge the injustice which
leads to poor health

And shorter lives for so many of us,

And may we build a society in which all
people can flourish.

NOTES

1. All World Website, *Tory peer says UK is becoming a fat nation that will bankrupt the NHS*: https://allworldreport.com/world-news/tory-peer-says-uk-becoming-fat-nation-will-bankrupt-nhs/

2. Decca Aikenhead, 'Peter Hitchens: "I don't believe in addiction. People take drugs because they enjoy it"', *Guardian* https://www.theguardian.com/books/2012/oct/21/peter-hitchens-addiction-drugs-war

3. Public Health England, *Chapter 5 Inequalities in Health, in Health Profile in England 2018*: https://www.gov.uk/government/publications/health-profile-for-england-2018/chapter-5-inequalities-in-health

4. Kate Pickett and Richard Wilson, 'A 25-year gap between life expectancy of rich and poor Londoners is a further indictment of our society', *Independent*, https://www.independent.co.uk/voices/comment/a-25-year-gap-between-the-life-expectancy-of-rich-

and-poor-londoners-is-a-further-indictment-of-our-9061888.html

5. ONS report *Health state life expectancies by national deprivation deciles, England and Wales: 2015-2017* Office for National Statistics: https://www.ons.gov.uk/peoplepopulationandcommunity/healthandsocialcare/healthinequalities/bulletins/healthstatelifeexpectanciesbyindexofmultiple-deprivationimd/2015to2017

6. Courtney Scott, Jennifer Sutherland, Anna Taylor, *Affordability of the UK's Eatwell Guide*, The Food Foundation, September 2018: http://foodfoundation.org.uk/publication/affordability-eatwell-guide/

7. NPC website, *Where are England's charities?*: https://www.thinknpc.org/resource-hub/where-are-englands-charities/

8. Combat Stress Website, *Veterans with alcohol problems are putting off seeking help*: https://www.cobseo.org.uk/mental-health-charity-combat-stress-finds-veterans-alcohol-addiction-putting-off-seeking-help-sixties/

9. Christiane Sanderson, Chip Somers, Clarinda Cuppage, *Numbing the Pain: Survivors' voices of childhood sexual abuse and addiction*, One In Four, March 2019: https://www.oneinfour.org.uk/numbing-the-pain-making-the-link-between-childhood-sexual-abuse-and-addiction/

10. *Ibid.*

11. Susan Ferreira, 'Portugal's radical drug policy is working: Why hasn't the world copied it?', *Guardian*, 5 December 2017: https://www.theguardian.com/

news/2017/dec/05/portugals-radical-drugs-policy-is-working-why-hasnt-the-world-copied-it

12. BBC News, *Drug deaths saw to highest level on record*, BBC website, 15 August 2019: https://www.bbc.co.uk/news/uk-49357077

13. United Nations Environmental Programme, *Air pollution hurts the poorest most*, 9 May 2019: https://www.unenvironment.org/news-and-stories/story/air-pollution-hurts-poorest-most

CONCLUSION

> 'For I was hungry and you gave me
> food, I was thirsty and you gave
> me drink, I was a stranger and you
> welcomed me, needing clothes and you
> clothed me, sick and you visited me, in
> prison and you came to see me.' Then
> the righteous will say to him in reply,
> 'Lord, when did we see you hungry and
> feed you, or thirsty and give you drink?
> When did we see you a stranger and
> welcome you, needing clothes and we
> clothed you? When did we see you sick
> or in prison and go to you?' And the
> King will answer, 'Amen I say to you, in
> so far as you did this to one of the least
> of these brothers or sisters of mine, you
> did it to me.'
>
> *Matthew 25:35-41*

This passage from Matthew could not be clearer.
Jesus instructs us to care for everyone in need –
to feed the hungry, visit the sick and welcome
the stranger. And importantly, I think, visiting
prisoners is included in this instruction, which
indicates that we must not limit our care to the

socially acceptable, those of whom the tabloids would approve. No, we must care for all people, without exception. People whom society may condemn, or regard as being of little value or importance are brothers and sisters of Jesus, and when we care for them we are caring for him.

Although the UK is often referred to as a Christian country, in too many ways we are failing to carry out this simple instruction from Jesus, to care for everyone. I write this conclusion haunted by thoughts of Errol Graham, a disabled man with a long history of mental distress, who starved to death when his disability benefits were stopped. Errol weighed 28.5kg (four-and-a-half stone) when his body was found by bailiffs who had knocked down his front door to evict him.[1] Errol joins a long list of dead disabled people who simply could not survive a system which is now too often callous and punitive towards those most in need of sensitivity and compassion.[2]

Of course, many Christians are doing the best they can to prevent such tragedies, but for people like Errol, charity can never be an adequate substitute for a decent, respectful system of social security, backed by properly resourced mental health services and social care.

Unfortunately, this shocking treatment of disabled people rarely if ever gets to the top of the political and news agenda – but the way we respond to refugees, asylum seekers and migrants has been a high-profile and contentious political issue in recent years. In our passage from Matthew, Jesus instructs us to welcome the stranger, but as Denise Cottrell-Boyce notes in her companion Bible study guide on this theme,[3] the responsibility for this has been largely placed onto the shoulders of the poorest people, both nationally and globally.

While refugees allowed to enter the UK are sent to already struggling poorer communities, the majority of refugees globally are hosted by poorer nations, with countries like Pakistan and Lebanon playing host to millions.[4] This has caused Amnesty International to dub the refugee crisis 'a global solidarity crisis', as many of the richest people and countries fail to share what they have with people who are desperately fleeing conflict and the effects of climate breakdown.[5] Within the UK, this solidarity crisis could also be said to have extended to disabled people.

Looking back over this book, it strikes me that perhaps what we all need to do is look beyond appearances in our communities and think a little more about what people's lives may really be like. The person who is considered such a good person because they have been caring for a family member without a break for years – are they really cheerful and coping, as they would like you to think, or are they exhausted and clinging on desperately, with no help available?

The person with a learning disability – have they got enough food in their cupboards, and can they afford to put their heating on? The person with a chronic illness who rarely gets out of the house – are they able to have a shower and a freshly cooked meal, or are they dependent on brief visits from a carer who has time to make them a sandwich or help them to the toilet, but nothing more? And what kind of a society are we living in, that these issues are real problems for millions of people?

Whether facing the challenges of illness, disability, caring, homelessness, poverty or exile, life for some people can be almost unbearably difficult and challenging. But it can be made much easier if we all look after each other in the way Jesus instructs us to do. And if we do this, we will not only be making life easier for each other, we will be serving him.

But it is surely not enough to show God's love through our personal, local efforts, whilst allowing to continue the national policies which cause such suffering in the first place. It is like the old story of the babies in the river, famously quoted by Archbishop Desmond Tutu. Imagine you and a group of friends are on the banks of a river, and you see a baby in the water. You would rush to save the baby. But another baby floats towards you, then another, and another. The babies keep coming. You frantically try to organise yourselves to rescue every baby as it floats downstream. Sooner or later, somebody needs to run upstream, and try to stop the babies entering the water.[6]

A society built on the values of Jesus would see nobody entering the water – nobody going without the necessities of life, and nobody desperate for want of company or practical assistance – least of all people who are already facing the challenges of illness and disability. If we truly see every person as being the equivalent of Jesus, then we will not rest until we know that every single person is guaranteed, by right, the support and care that we would wish to show to him.

And for all who are presently suffering, I hope that this book will have helped in some small way to make you feel that you do not suffer alone, even if human beings are currently letting you down terribly. You are unique, and as valuable as any human being who ever lived. God knows and understands your suffering and is with you in solidarity. What we need now is for our society to embrace that solidarity and make it manifest through compassionate policies, adequate resources, and sensitive implementation.

As noted above, this book is paired with another in the series by Denise Cottrell-Boyce, about welcoming the stranger.[7] I recently heard a story about a nativity play which I think is relevant to both this book and Denise's, and which models the radically inclusive love which Jesus showed and asks us to show. In this nativity play, a boy with Downs syndrome had been cast as the innkeeper. Joseph and Mary approached the inn and knocked on the door, and the boy's big moment arrived. It wasn't clear whether he'd forgotten his lines, or just decided to ignore the script and follow his instincts, but he opened the door, stretched out his arms and said, with a big smile, 'Come in, there's plenty of room.' That's the kind of society the early Christian communities were striving to be, and it's the kind of society we should be striving to create.

NOTES

1. John Pring, 'The death of Errol Graham: Man starved to death after DWP wrongly stopped his benefits', *Disability News Service*, 23 January 2020: https://www.disabilitynewsservice.com/errol-graham-legal-challenge-exposes-years-of-dwp-dishonesty-and-broken-promises/

2. John Pring, 'DWP: The case for the prosecution' *Disability News Service*, 2 December 2019: https://www.disabilitynewsservice.com/dwp-the-case-for-the-prosecution/

3. Denise Cottrell-Boyce, *How the Bible Can Help Us Understand Welcoming the Stranger* (Darton, Longman and Todd, 2020)

4. Charlotte Edmonds, '84 per cent of refugees live in developing countries.' *World Economic Forum Website* 20 June 2017. https://www.weforum.org/agenda/2017/06/eighty-four-percent-of-refugees-live-in-developing-countries/

5. Amnesty International website. *The world's refugees in numbers*. https://www.amnesty.org/en/what-we-do/refugees-asylum-seekers-and-migrants/global-refugee-crisis-statistics-and-facts/

6. Unitarian Universalist Association, *Babies in the Water*: http://www.windmillsonline.co.uk/there-comes-a-point-where-we-need-to-stop-just-pulling-people-out-of-the-river-we-need-to-go-upstream-and-find-out-why-theyre-falling-in/

7. Denise Cottrell-Boyce, *How the Bible Can Help Us Understand Welcoming the Stranger* (Darton, Longman and Todd, 2020)

ACKNOWLEDGEMENTS

I am very grateful to my husband Jim, whose moral and practical support made it possible for me to complete this project.

I am also very grateful to my friend Jill Segger, who has been so supportive and encouraging. Being able to discuss this project with her has been invaluable.

In writing this book I became even more conscious of how lucky I have been to be part of such a loving and caring family. To say thank you doesn't seem enough, but I hope they all know how much they are appreciated.

I have to make special mention of my mum, Sheila Connolly. Widowed in her thirties, she brought up a young family alone without complaint or self-pity and set me an extremely impressive example of love and courage.

This book is dedicated to the memory of Liam Carter.